THURSDAYS '

Dear Penny,

Well, I don't suppose anything I have to say will stop you. But why do you want to put your loved ones on the spot by printing our letters? Certainly you better get Aunt Amey's and Gran's permission, and you have your lawyer friend, Darwin, fine tooth your book for legal reasons. I don't want to have that responsibility on my back. I hope what I said in those letters won't embarrass anyone—including me. And you better be mighty careful about what you say about your boss and that nice lady you don't like—Mrs. Montenegro. You may find yourself out on the street with no job.

What does the title mean? Thursdays 'til 9? I never heard of a book called that. I like one word titles like Giant, the Bible and Beowulf. I can remember them. I sure hope you show some sense of breeding and there are no sex scenes. That would be the end. And I hope you aren't going into all that business about the fairy you hired or that orangutang that went berserk at your fashion show.

Let me know when the book comes out, so I can have a little "do" and ask Mr. Reynoldson, Gran and Aunt Amey over. Can you send me about twelve

copies for the neighbors? I still can't fathom filling up a whole book on your work for a year in that strange department store. But I'll take it on faith.

Love,
Mother

BY JANE TRAHEY

Jane Trahey on Women and Power
Life with Mother Superior
Taste of Texas
One Hundred Years of Harper's Bazaar
Pecked to Death by Goslings
Ring Round the Bathtub *(a play)*

Thursdays 'til 9

A NOVEL BY

JANE TRAHEY

HARCOURT BRACE JOVANOVICH

NEW YORK AND LONDON

Requests for permission to make copies of
any part of the work should be mailed to
Permissions, Harcourt Brace Jovanovich, Inc.
757 Third Avenue, New York, N.Y. 10017

Graphic Designs by Susan Clifton
Illustrations by Bette Fraser

Printed in the United States of America

LIBRARY OF CONGRESS CATALOGING IN PUBLICATION DATA
Trahey, Jane.
Thursdays 'til 9.
I. Title.
PZ4.T7645Th   [PS3570.R3]   813'.54   79-3366
ISBN 0-15-190261-5

First edition
B C D E

For Mama

The author is grateful for
permission to use the logos
from Marshall Field & Co.,
Carson Pirie Scott & Co.,
and Neiman-Marcus;
and
to Carol Channing for wearing
the famed Sablinka, and to
Tom John who found my
perceptive editor,
Marcia Magill.

Penelope Smith
8518 W. Winston Drive
Chicago, Illinois 60611

March 15, 1979

Mr. John Burke, Chairman
B. Altman & Co.
Fifth Ave. at 34th St.
New York, N.Y. 10016

Dear Mr. Burke,

Your advertising is most intriguing. From out here in Second City I literally drool for your kind of copy slants. Do you, would you ever consider hiring a writer from old Windy City?

I've been a copywriter at Carson Pirie Scott & Co. for two years, and I've had a hand in writing about everything. Recently I was appointed Copy Chief, and now I am responsible for corporate advertising as well. I really enjoy this facet of advertising and feel that the average retailer does too little of this kind of image building.

I have a B.A. degree from Excelsior in Communications ('76) and I did some graduate work at Wisconsin in Existential Philosophy. Unfortunately, Simone de Beauvoir has this area tied up. I'm a young 25 (which is like saying a "full gallon"). I'm not married and money isn't the only thing I'll work for. I have to make just enough to live a nice, exciting life in the big A.

I am enclosing a batch of stats of my work which will give you an idea of the quality of my endeavors for Carson's. I look forward to hearing from you should you have any openings.

Sincerely,

Penelope Smith

enc: 20 stats

Penelope Smith
8518 W. Winston Drive
Chicago, Illinois 60611

March 16, 1979

Mr. Ira Neimark, President
Bergdorf Goodman
Fifth Ave. at 58th St.
New York, N.Y. 10019

Dear Mr. Neimark,

It's come to my attention that you are on a search for a creative director for your promotion and advertising. I'd most certainly like to be considered for the post. Here's why.

For the past two years I have been Copy Chief on all fashion and cosmetic copy at Carson Pirie Scott & Co. There isn't much in the store I haven't had some crack at in writing. Recently I have become more and more involved in institutional advertising. But frankly, I like the excitement of the fashion/cosmetic world. (I'm pure WWD.)

I have a B.A. in English from Excelsior College and did graduate work at Wisconsin in Costume Design.

I'm enclosing a collection of my recent work in the store that I particularly like. A while back I saw a whole newspaper you did every couple of weeks for your White Plains store--wow, it's smashing!

Currently I'm drawing 18 G's and am due for a sizable increase. However, I feel that my growth should be in a more sophisticated city and store. If you need a good writer, I'd love an interview.

Sincerely,

Penelope Smith

enc: 15 full-page stats

Penelope Smith
8518 W. Winston Drive
Chicago, Illinois 60611

March 19, 1979

Dear Ms. Stegner,

Recently I read of your appointment as President of the fine old store, Harzfeld's. I was thrilled that a woman got the job (12,000 retail establishments--now, 4 female presidents!). Shows you what fantastic strides women are making (she said facetiously). This leaves me 11,996 posts to try for. But I've got a way to go.

I was very interested in your plans to update the store and make it the best in the Midwest, and I think I could help you do just that. I'm a copy-writer at Carson Pirie Scott & Co., and I will undoubtedly be a copywriter here for the next 20 years if I don't get going. Would you consider (provided you like the work I'm sending) giving me a chance to try for your ad manager job?

My education goes like this. I have a double major from Excelsior College in English/Philosophy. But the market for philosophers dried up sometime in the 17th century. However, I do believe there is still a place for someone who can write a complete sentence and parse it properly.

I have no attachments other than my mother and her Chow dog, and they have both made it clear to me that they would love to have a place to visit out of town. I'd like to work in a store enlightened enough to have a woman at the top.

Sincerely,

Penelope Smith

enc: 13 photostats of current work

Penelope Smith
8518 W. Winston Drive
Chicago, Illinois 60611

March 21, 1979

Mr. Harold Nevins
Nevins Markham
Elm and Orchard
Canyon City, Tex. 78254

Dear Mr. Nevins,

Your advertising is simply great! From out here in Second City I literally drool over it. Do you, would you, could you ever find space for me? Currently I'm the Assistant Advertising Manager at Carson Pirie Scott & Co., but I'm not title hungry. I'd rather work in an exciting ambience than have an exciting title in a department store atmosphere.

I have my B.A. from Excelsior in Chinese History (I understand you've been marketing Chinese merchandise very well these days), and I did a good bit of work at Wisconsin on my master's in Communications.

As for fashion writing, I've done my homework, i.e., Bill Blass, Calvin Klein, Krizia, Laug, Armani, etc. (ads enclosed). Image making, community interest advertising, and corporate ad thinking are all joys to work on. Money means nothing to me, although I'm growing to like it more and more. All I need is enough for a gorgeous adobe hacienda and the good life in Canyon City. I hope you are in the market for a me.

Sincerely,

Penelope Smith

enc: 27 photostats
1 personality picture profile

A Rare Portrait of Penelope Smith at Ease

Color: Nice & Easy (100)

Adrien Arpel's Make-over face

Blue eyes Sparkling

Mono Shadow

Styling by S

Lamy pen

Missoni top

Elsa Peretti's sterling twist

Heart of Gold

Jaeger jacket

Jaeger trousers

Ward Bennett chair

18th century porcelain cage (no bird)

Hermès carry-all

Ferragamos firmly on the ground.

Penelope Smith
8518 W. Winston Drive
Chicago, Illinois 60611

APPLICATIONS SENT AND CROSS-REFERENCE CHECKS

Answ.	Store	Pres.	Specialty	Stats
	Altman 3/15	Burke	copy corp. adv. BA--Comm. Grad--Phil.	United Fund, Cerebral P., new store (9), Christmas, item stack ads (6), men's sale, radio commercials
	Bergdorf 3/16	Neimark	fashion cosm. copy BA--Eng. Grad--Cost. Des.	Blass, Laug, Krizia, Basile, Armani, Arden, Trigère, asst. item ads (5), Fendi bags, Bagheera bags, Sanchez bags
	Harzfeld's 3/19	Stegner	fashion copy dbl. maj. Phil./Eng.	Lauren book, cosmetics (6), Anne Klein, R. Lauren, Missoni, London Fog, Burberry, Jourdan Shoe ad in French
	Nevins 3/21	Nevins	fashion image BA--Chinese Hist. Grad--Comm.	Blass, Laug, Krizia, Chloé, Klein, Lauren, United Fund, new store (9), asst. item ads (9), jade jewelry, Chinese robe, antique booklet

Inter-Correspondence

March 26, 1979

to: Staff

from: Fred R. Runyon

re: Photostats

Despite the fact that I have requested
over and over again that the photostat
machine not be used without permission
from Irwin Glasser, it has once again
been brought to my attention that this
situation is completely out of hand. In
the past few weeks 75 full-page stats
were made without Mr. Glasser's knowl-
edge. Consequently I have instructed
Glasser to lock the production room at
all times unless there is some staff
member from the production department
present.

Photostats are very expensive and I must
account to management for every dollar
not budgeted. Needless to say, if I, or
Glasser, find out who is using the stat
machine, they will answer to me.

nevins markham

April 2, 1979

Take a look at the enclosed material from
a copywriter at Carson Pirie Scott & Co.
and let me know what you think. Her
grammar isn't exactly Oxford, but she has
a nice offbeat quality that might work
for us. And she has one terrific imag-
ination. For instance, she's just 25,
but she'd have to be well into her
forties to have accomplished what she
claims. I thought I'd see her in May when
I'm in Chicago. She could get started
now, get things going before Isabella
Montenegro comes in. It's the beginning
of the creative pyramid we've talked
about so many times. Provided she's
right, of course. What's your reaction to
the work?

HN/bb

nevins markham
elm and orchard
canyon city, texas 78254

office of the president

April 3, 1979

Ms. Penelope Smith
8518 West Winston Drive
Chicago, Illinois 60611

Dear Ms. Smith,

Thanks so much for sending along all the
interesting materials. I was very impressed with your portfolio. I'm going
to be in Chicago on Wednesday, May 9.
You can call me at the Ritz and we'll
make an appointment to meet.

I'll have some time in the morning, so
if you can block off an hour or so we can
confirm the time by phone.

Sincerely,

Harold Nevins
President

HN/bb

nevins markham

May 4, 1979

These aren't exactly what I'd call glowing recommendations, but I've never claimed I knew what you looked for in the advertising department. Do you want me to forget the whole thing?

enc: 2 recommendations re Penelope Smith

PLEASE ADDRESS REPLY TO:

One South State Street
Chicago, Illinois 60603

April 27, 1979

Ms. Ada Pump
Personnel Director
Nevins Markham
Elm and Orchard
Canyon City, Texas 78254

Dear Ms. Pump,

We have searched our records and are happy to inform you that Ms. Penelope Smith has been in our Advertising Department as a Junior Copywriter for the past two years. Mr. Runyon, our Advertising Director, says that she was punctual and performed her duties adequately. I hope this will be of help in screening.

Sincerely,

E. Dodson
Personnel Department

Excelsior College
Chippewa Falls, Wisconsin 54729

Office of the Dean

May 1, 1979

Ms. Ada Pump
Personnel Department
Nevins Markham
Elm & Orchard
Canyon City, Texas 78254

Dear Ms. Pump,

Ms. Penelope Smith has asked that I write
a recommendation for her. Ms. Smith
attended Excelsior College from 1972 to
1976 and graduated in June '76. She
majored in English Literature and
completed her credits for a minor in
Philosophy. The faculty remember her well
for her participation on The Banner (our
student newspaper) and for her satirical
pieces reflecting student life at
Excelsior. I hope she will prove to be a
good employee in your store.

Sincerely,

Catharine Matson
Dean

CM/lb

Inter-Correspondence

May 8, 1979

To   Fred R. Runyon

From Penelope Smith

Re   Wisdom Tooth

I hope it is OK if I come in late tomorrow
morning as I have to have a tooth pulled
and it was the only time the dentist
could fit me in. Yours in deep pain.

nevins markham
elm and orchard
canyon city, texas 78254

office of the president

May 14, 1979

Ms. Penelope Smith
8518 West Winston Drive
Chicago, Illinois 60611

Dear Ms. Smith,

This will confirm, per our telephone conversation
of May 11, 1979, that you will join Nevins Markham
as of June 4, 1979, in the capacity of Assistant
Advertising Manager. Although I was under the
impression that you were more interested in
exciting ambiences than in titles, I understand
your position and I am happy to bestow on you this
title. However, as you know, I expect you to assume
the duties of Copy Chief as well. The staff is small
and you will have to play many roles.

Since I'm aware of the high costs of moving to a new
city, I am enclosing an open airlines ticket. Let me
know when you are arriving and at what time, and I
will arrange for a member of the staff to meet you
at the airport. For the moment, my secretary, Ms.
Burns, has booked a room for you at the Buena Vista
Hotel. I believe it will fit your needs until you
find an apartment.

We are looking forward to having you on our
promotion staff and I hope we will have a long and
mutually rewarding relationship.

Sincerely yours,

Harold Nevins
President

cc: Sue Ellen Anderson, Public Relations

enc: airlines ticket

HN/bb

Inter-Correspondence

May 17, 1979

to: Fred Runyon

from: Penelope Smith

I tried to find you yesterday to tell you
the good news but alas! You were locked
in the photostat room.

The news--I've been discovered by Harold
Nevins. And I'm going to go work at
Nevins Markham as "Assistant Advertising
Manager." If it's OK with you I'd like to
leave on May 31. I've had a good time
working here with you and I appreciate
all your teaching time. Thanks much.

P.S. Is it OK if I make some stats of a
few of the best ads I did here? Should I
ask Irwin too?

Inter-Correspondence

May 18, 1979

To: Penelope Smith

From: Fred Runyon

OK for the 31st. OK for the stats. And
when did you bother asking before? Good
luck and I'm proud of you.

60610 MR TS CHICAGO ILL 5-28 4.30P CST
HAROLD NEVINS
NEVINS MARKHAM
CANYON CITY, TX 78254
ARRIVE JUNE 2 AMERICAN AIRLINES FLT 109 AT
1:51 PM. LEAVE BEREFT CARSON'S DESOLATE
FAMILY, LACHRYMOSE FRIENDS. PENELOPE SMITH

From the desk of

Sue Ellen Anderson
Public Relations/Nevins Markham

May 16, 1979

To: Harold Nevins

I'll go get Penelope Smith myself. After
Harriet Horspant, your last bottom of the
pyramid, I wouldn't miss this for the
world--even on a Saturday afternoon. Let
me know what plane to meet.

nevins markham

June 4, 1979

Lord, you were nice to pick me up on such
a red-hot Saturday. I appreciate it and
the wonderful Mexie lunch. (Is it always
so hot?) The Buena Vista is really nice,
but I'd really like to find a small
furnished apartment where I could stow
some tuna and Cokes. Eating out is too
expensive for my budget. Later on I can
get my own stuff and settle down.

Buena Vista Hotel 106 Market, Canyon City, Texas 78254

June 5, 1979

Dear Mama,

After talking to you Sunday night I really had
the blues. But since then I haven't had time to even
think about being away. I can't believe I'm here--
that is, until I hit the sunshine. Boy, is it hot
here! But I do like the job--so far. I'm working my
tail off. If this continues you will have to stop
saying I'm too lazy to work and too nervous to
steal!
Mr. Nevins is just great. I have an office
that's small but it's right out of Architectural
Digest. The Texans are so sweet I suspect them. They
keep saying, "You-all hurry back, honey" and "You-
all have a niaaaaaace day." The one thing I hate--
living in a hotel. As soon as I get a second I'm
going apartment shopping. I hear they are hard to
find and expensive and you gotta take 'em for two
years. What if I don't dig it here? What if they
don't dig me here? After a year or so I'd like to
build a house.
Actually, I'm not chic enough for this place.
Everywhere I look I see Missonis, Armanis, Fendis,
Basiles, or Versachis. All the buyers look like
they're done by Trigère. I'll have to dude up more
and that will cost me, too. I've made one nice
friend. She's the PR director AND she has a car.
This is vital in Canyon City. They never heard of
buses. Mercedes and Rolls are a dime a dozen. Even
though I can walk to work, this place is rolled up
at 6 P.M. It looks like La Salle Street on Sunday.
Start planning a visit. I miss you something
fierce. Give my love to Gran and Auny Amey. Did you
know Gran shoved a bag of bananas at me just before
I boarded the plane? I smelled up the whole tourist
section. Anyway, I miss all of you, or should I say
"you-all," including Pineapple Whip, that hairy
beast of yours. I've got to quit now. I want to
write Darwin before I fall asleep. Write lots. Love,
Penny

Buena Vista Hotel 106 Market, Canyon City, Texas 78254

June 5, 1979

Dearest Darwin,

Oh, Dar! I miss you! I knew I would. But I didn't ever have a clue how much. (And I've only been here four days!) I tried not to sound too morose on the phone but I am lonely. I am homesick. I even miss Gran and Amey. Could you believe Aunt Amey chasing me down the boarding ramp shouting, "Eat your bananas before they get black!" That's real cachet! All'I can say is thank God she wasn't at the other end. When I got off the plane there stood Sue Ellen Anderson, the Public Relations Director. She was wearing a smashingly beautiful beige silk dress and there was not one wrinkle in it. I wondered if she had dressed at the airport.

The weather here is ungodly. It's so hot it's like trying to live in the Gary Indiana steel mills. I got palm burns just trying to open Sue Ellen's car door. And then didn't she whisk me off to a Mexican restaurant for hot tamales. I think I'll take Gran's advice and wear wet lettuce leaves under my hat. That would help my image here at Nevins Markham.

Sue Ellen is really nice. She's tiny. Has dark curly hair and the bone structure of a myna bird. I would guess she's kind of in her mid- to late thirties. She told me she has worked here since the day she graduated from U. of Missouri. Started as a secretary. (What else for a female college grad?)

She finally deposited me at the Hotel Buena Vista. My vista being an insurance company office. Lots of old ladies live here. They sit in the lobby all day and well into the night. I can hardly wait to lose this place and get a pad of my own and get you down here!

Well, you must hear about my first days in

Nevinsland. First off, I met the ad production guy. His name is Bill Lance. He's tall, taciturn, and very Texan. (Forgive the alliteration.) He does traffic, mail, announcements, production, mailing pieces, etc. He's good. He wears Lauren jeans, Lauren boots, and plenty of silver and turquoise jewelry. What am I to think of that? There is just one artist. Her name is Stella Branden. She is very, very good. She is into all the new fashion and her idol is Lulu de la Falaise from W. You know, the chic-eee who had the funny wedding with swans, etc. Well, Stella is swathed in glamour and sits at her drawing board devouring French Vogue and sipping espresso which she brews for herself.

Sue Ellen waltzed me around the store to meet the key people. First up--Ethle Sideman. No, I didn't spell Ethel wrong. Her name is ETH-LEE. She buys better dresses. Doesn't this tell you that somewhere in this store someone sells worser dresses? Ethle wore thousands of pounds of gold. Bracelets, baubles, pins, rings. She looks like a walking Van Cleef and Arpels. Sue Ellen says that every time her husband plays around he buys her a "gilt/guilt" present. He must be a sex fiend. Anyway, she showed me a little Halston number that had just arrived and she said, "My philosophy is that of Halston. I think enough is toooo much." She thought a minute. "No, not enough is too much! No, too much is not enough. You know what I mean?" I didn't. But old Halston must understand that enough is too much. The number was priced at 900 bucks.

And then into my life came Tiny Halmark, who buys coats. She has streaked ash-blond hair with a special pink rinse. She puffed her way through 12 menthol lights in 15 minutes. Incidentally, all the

3.

buyers' offices are right smack in the middle of
their merchandise bins. It seems that Mr. N. has a
philosophy that you sell what you see every day. The
buyers here do not live "over" the store. Tiny was
counting cashmere wrap coats. She looked up and
never stopped counting during our conversation.
"Thirteen, fourteen, listen, darling, I am glad
you're here. You come from Carson's. It's a nice
place. Let me tell you they are merchants. Here
you'll earn every dollar you make. Sixteen,
seventeen, eighteen. You have to stretch every
dollar and still cover the bases and still be chic,
nineteen, twenty. I only bought twelve of this coat.
I definitely remember buying only twelve of this
coat and now, my God, there are twenty. There must
be a male coat in this bin. Don't ask me why I'm
here buying coats in a climate like this. There is
no reason for a coat. Maybe Arafat or the Ayatollah
would like a cashmere coat but no one else wants
one. I tell Abe Schrader, Abe, for the love of God,
make me light coats. Make me silk coats. Linen
coats. Cotton coats. But oh, no, he's into Berber
wools."

Sue Ellen rescued me and whisked me off to
meet the display director (who is neat) and the shoe
buyer (who is nuts) and a real countess who buys for
a shop called the "Collectors." I peeked at a
couple of price tags and I think the store must have
a deal with Sotheby's for auctions. She kissed me on
both cheeks and said, "Sherry, Sherry" a lot.

So now you know some of the characters. I got
to tell you I felt like Heidi just down from
Grandpa's mountain where I had been out with the
goats. Darling, my fingers are getting paralyzed. I
got to get to bed so I can get up early and prepare

my ice pack for the morning walk. Golly damn, I miss you. Why can't you be a Canyon City attorney? Night, love.

    Penny

P.S. Please read these society clips from the Sunday paper.

Emma Bawden Bride of Harold Steineke

Miss Emma Bawden became the bride of Harold Steineke on Thursday, May 31, at a ceremony held in the Lutheran Pentecostal Church of the Living Savior. Mr. Harris Bawden, the bride's brother and pastor of the church, joined them in holy wedlock. The bride wore white satin and carried a white leather-covered Bible topped with Stephanotis. The groom and groomsmen wore bachelor buttons in their bottom holes.

Ladies' Drum and Bugle Corps Reunites

A reunion was scheduled for the Ladies' Drum and Bugle Corps of Fort Worth for June 9, Mrs. Hannah Ericson announced today. It will be held at the Wylie Beach and will replace the Corps annual cockout.

nevins markham

June 8, 1979

I know you have your hands full getting settled, but I do want you to get started thinking about Christmas and next spring. We're already late for Christmas. I want you to bead in on the holiday especially before you get bogged down with too many other problems.

As you know, Mrs. Isabella Montenegro will be joining us early in July as our new Sales Promotion Vice-President, and I'd like to have some things lined up for her to edit. I think we'll have a much more stimulating meeting when she comes if we have a lot of ideas to knock around.

The philosophy of Nevins Markham on Christmas, for example, is to avoid at all costs any Christmas cliché. No reindeer or Santas, etc. However, we don't want to get so stratospheric that we do nothing to attract Mr. and Mrs. Canyon City. There are lots of people who will buy a $15 present just to get the Nevins Markham gift wrap. Ask Sue Ellen to show you the clip book on the publicity we get just on gift wraps.

Our image is a tough one. You have to walk a tightrope. We want to be sophisticated enough to attract the press and the knowledgeable shopper, but we never want to lose sight of the "just folks" category.

Last Christmas we had a children's zoo. We had baby animals from all over the world. We did an "Animal

inter-office memo

to: Penelope Smith

from: Harold Nevins

page 2

Crackers Christmas" and we worked our way in merchandising all through the store. The gourmet shop did giant animal cracker cookies. We did sheets. We did shirtings. We made spreads for kids' beds. We did children's toys, clothes, charms, etc. Besides being successful as a PR gimmick, it sold a lot of merchandise. However, I caution you on live animals. They're a lot of work. TJ Bennis can show you window displays and interior displays.

For spring I want something that will bring people in to just "gawk." So see what you can get going for these two major promos.

HN/bb

From the desk of

Sue Ellen Anderson
Public Relations/Nevins Markham

June 8, 1979

To: Penny Smith

I clipped this from the Sunday paper.
Maybe you could case them some evening.
Also, I checked around and one of the
salespeople in Designer Sportswear has a
sister who has a guest cottage. Her name
is Mrs. Gundeson and her phone is KL 5-
6758. If this isn't right I'll drive you
around on Saturday. Meanwhile, how about
dinner Wed.? You'll get too attached to
room service if you don't get out.

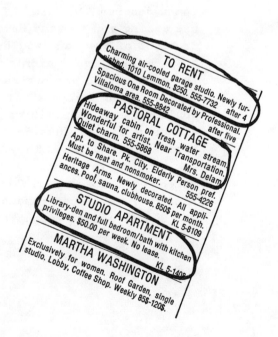

Marshall Field & Company

Sunday the 10th

Dear Penelope,

In case you're wondering where on earth I got
this stationery, I got it in Aunt Amey's department
yesterday when I stopped by to see her and she was
out. I remember when Field's used to have a writing
room right alongside the toilets. You got all the
free stationery and envelopes you wanted, and you
could spend the day there writing your letters and
paying your bills. But that day is gone forever.
First the linen towels went. Then the writing room.
Then the paper. Well, I just took a stack and tucked
it in my bag--in honor of the good old days. I used
to have some nice personalized stationery of my own
with Chinese monograms on it, but I don't write to
anyone but the People's Gas and Light and they sure
don't deserve that kind of swank. It's certainly no
use asking you to send Nevins Markham paper as it's
from out of town and wouldn't do me much good.

Believe me, I didn't say a word to Gran about
the bananas. It was her way of saying, "Bon
Voyage." Don't look a gift horse in the mouth.
You're always complaining about cramps in your
arches so it wouldn't do you any harm to eat a
banana now and then. They are filled with potassium.

I know you ignore advice but take it from
someone who loves you. Don't get yourself into any
kind of lease. Just remember poor Mrs. Butler after
Mr. Butler passed away. Why don't you find yourself

2.

a couple of nice rooms and get a lot of ferns for
the windows? Ferns have a way of cheering up a room
like nothing else in the world. And they're not hard
to conquer at all. You don't have to lavish love on
a fern like you do on a bromeliad.

    In your letter you mentioned a lot of Ital-
ians. I didn't know there were a lot of Italians
in Texas. However, I have always found them to be
nice, warm people. I showed your letter to Aunt Amey
and she thought the names seemed familiar. Thought
they were clothes designers but said they didn't
live in Texas. They live in Italy. So you must be
mistaken. Nothing new here. I'm cooking lamb and
Gran and Amey are coming. Pineapple likes the scraps
but I'm not a lamb person. Love,

                Mother

nevins markham

inter-office memo

to: Bill Lance, Production

from: Penny Smith

June 11, 1979

Would it be a lot of bucks to have 500
sheets of the attached memo pad done for
me? It's my own design and I'd like to
have something special. How about eating
with me tomorrow or the next day?

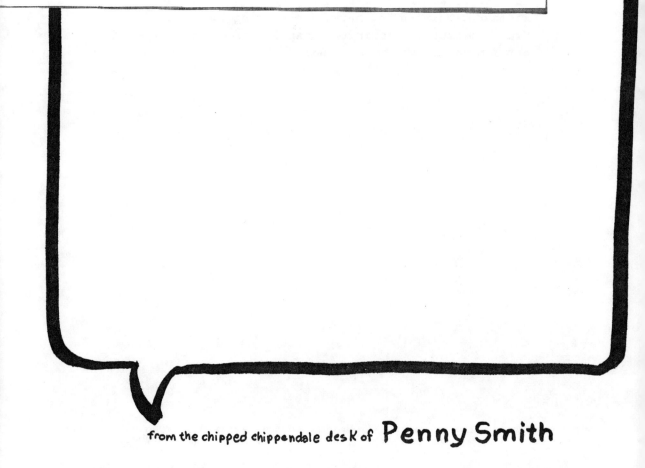

from the chipped chippendale desk of Penny Smith

Sunday night

Dear Dar,

Well, I have cased more damn water holes being
advertised as apartments than you can shake a stick
at. You cannot believe what people have for rent.
Everything I saw today can be categorized in one of
three ways. Bat. Cat. Rat.

The first one I checked out was a "pastoral
cottage." It was pastoral all right. The lady who
advertised it was having supper on her front porch.
She had no teeth. She introduced me to her friend
Mizzhurson. This is Texan for Mrs. Harrison. After
she had gummed several chops she asked Mizzhurson to
pass the "maters." This is Texan for tomatoes.
Finally she heaved her body out of her chair and
grabbed the broom. We walked down a swampy path in
the back of her overgrown garden. "My husbind used
to lak to sit back here and thank. He was a real
thanker." At that she broomed down the door of an
old outbuilding. The door was covered with cobwebs.
From the swamp down I knew it was a waste of time. I
told her it was much too big for me. Too grand for
me. Too much for me. She paid no attention. "Doan
you-all be fraid of these here little ole bats. They
are more afraid of you. They are theeee best
assurance that you will have real quiet. Bats don't
never roost nowheres there's noise."

~~delete pastoral cottage~~

On to the garage apartment. The house in front
was early Norman Conquest. The front door to the
house was open. I poked my head in and called out. A
woman shouted, "Don't let the cat out!" I hadn't
seen any cat. Then a huge black lump the size of a
watermelon dropped out of the heavens into my arms.
Obviously, he lived in the light fixture. Lady
appeared wearing a Bill Tice Production No. She took
the cat from my fearfully frozen arms. "Naughty

Foster," she cooed at the cat. "Foster wants to play pat-a-cake." (Have you ever played pat-a-cake with a strange cat?) And did Foster ever play! After several rounds and a few scratches, she locked up Foster and we climbed up a flight of stairs next to her garage. The temperature hovered around 100 (31 celsius). But that was nothing to what the temperature was in the little dahlin' apartment. "I thought you said it was air-cooled," I snarled. "Why, it is air-cooled! Some nights it's so cool you need a cover. Too cold for Foster some nights."

delete air-cooled garage *e*

Next--the rat lady's pad. Dark and shaded living room. Blinds drawn tight. When rat lady flicked on the lights I saw a row of twenty knight's heads. They were armor. They had been wired for light and their mouths slowly opened, revealing 20-watt yellow bulbs. Her husband (God rest his good soul) had collected armor. The rooms I would occupy are the repository of his knights-in-armor collection. A super place for me to study and work on gloomy days, provided I changed my name to Aquitaine.

delete library den

So I'm still roomless in Gaza. But Sue Ellen says Mrs. Gundeson's sister is waiting for me. She's a night nurse and her husband is a fireman. He works every other day. If only you were here to laugh it wouldn't seem so depressing. Everything else is fine. Got to quit now and write some crispy Seiko watch copy. I miss you. I miss you. I miss you. Take care and love from the homeless homesick.

Penny

From the desk of

Sue Ellen Anderson
Public Relations/Nevins Markham

2095958

June 18, 1979

To: Bob Sweeney, Mailing Lists

Can you get the following telegram out to the following people:

Grace Mae Condesta, _Canyon Herald_
Eliot Kyal, _Canyon City Clarion_
Melody Clivendon, _Houston Post_
Bobby Joe Westheim, _Houston Chronicle_
Myrna Swillett, _Women's Wear Daily Dallas_
Ellen Worth, _Texas Today_
Morton McAfee, WQUB-TV
Bea Fine, _Texas Monthly_

You are cordially invited to meet
Isabella Montenegro, our Vice-President
and Sales Promotion Director. Cocktails 5
to 7   Capricorn Room   Nevins Markham
June 29   RSVP   Sue Ellen Anderson
555-0500   ext. 150

June 17, 1979

to: Carson Pirie Scott Ad Department

from: Papillon Smith, author of
       How I Escaped from Fred R. Runyon

Many, many thanks for my wonderful send-off! I
loved my bracelet and I loved my Le Perroquet
lunch. A far cry from our Puss 'n Boot lunches at
the glorious employees' cafeteria. You are all
dolls. And the very fact that I could show my
mother a present finally convinced her that I
had not been fired.

I got to tell you that Harold Nevins is a swell
guy to work for. He looks like Rockford, only
older. The buyers are all bonkers, but what do
you expect from buyers? I have one new friend
who is great fun. She does PR. She also goes
right off the wall with one drink, which limits
my consumption enormously. I miss all of you.
Write to me. I even miss Fred R. Runyon if you
can believe it. How do you like my new stationery? It's posh, ain't it? Love,
                                    Penny

from the chipped chippendale desk of Penny Smith

CONSULAAT-GENERAAL DER HAGUE
Consulate General of the Hague

660 Madison Avenue
New York, N.Y. 10019
Tel: 212-555-1600
Telegr:adres: "Haglandia New York"

June 18, 1979

Ms. Penelope Smith
Advertising Manager
Nevins Markham
Elm and Orchard
Canyon City, Texas 78254

Dear Ms. Smith,

Thank you so much for your proposal of a
Netherlands promotion in your store. It is my desire
that we do participate, and we will do all that we
can to participate.

Mr. Ludwig Lebb, of Dutch Air, has already
indicated his keen interest in the project, and I
suggest that your first step be to contact him
directly in New York City.

I have been in touch with the Dutch Bulb
Growers Association, and Mr. Harvey Klahorn shows
great enthusiasm as well. You can reach him at 30
Rockefeller Plaza.

If there is anything we can do from this end to
help expand your promotional ideas, please do not
hesitate to contact me.

Very truly yours,

Volengen Hoort
Chargé

VH/bw

nevins markham

June 19, 1979

I hope everything is set for the Isabella
Montenegro press party. You'll be happy
to know that John Yonkaletch, publisher
of the Dallas Sun, and Liss Cobb III of the
Clarion are both coming. Obviously, our
new Sales Promotion Director has contacts
and clout. I know you'll be delighted
about that. She is then planning on going
to New York to wind up some business
matters and plans to be here full-time
after the 4th. She's expressed interest
in getting started on Christmas and
spring as quickly as possible and would
like to meet you both early on Friday
morning. She'll be at the Plaza
International.

HN/bb

DUTCH BULB GROWERS
(nothing like a Holland Tulip)

June 22, 1979

Ms. Penelope Smith
Advertising Manager
Nevins Markham
Elm and Orchard
Canyon City, Texas 78254

Dear Ms. Smith,

It was very pleasant talking with you last Wednesday. We are all very enthusiastic about the forthcoming Tulip-Netherlands promotion at your store. I am happy to tell you that my board has unanimously agreed to supply the store with 125,000 tulips. There will be at least 1,000 varieties, with emphasis on the Cottage and Darwin. As you suggested, we will try to send enough Darwin blacks to make a spectacular backdrop you can light at night. For your parrot jungle we'll have some self-colored parrots as well as the green and yellow stripings. Keep in mind, however, that the parrots are heavy and quite likely to droop. We'll also have quantities of Bizarres (the yellow marked with purple or red) and the Bybloemens, which are the whites marked with either purple or rose. There are no yellows in the Darwins. I particularly like the Van Thol tulip, which is scarlet with yellow edges.

To answer your question on the life span of a tulip after it opens, I'd say that if you keep the store cool (low 60s) a tulip should keep for five days. Your suggestion of starting with 75,000 and then filling in later with 50,000 which we will force-bloom makes great sense to us.

In Holland we say "Ya Ya" when everything goes right and I hope we will have many occasions to use this quaint old saying in our Nevins Markham promotion.

Sincerely,

Harvey Klahorn
Director

HK/ab

herengracht 392—amsterdam—telefoon 011-31-20 434355

June 23--and it's a beautiful
Saturday. Temp. 106

Dearest Darwin Tulip,

Did you know that there are thousands of tulip
varieties but that the most prestigious one of all is the
"Darwin"? I'm having the best time getting my tulip act
together. As soon as I get a second, I'm going to write up
a whole presentation for Harold Nevins. But I'm kind of
gun-shy of him. He's so bloody smart and chic. What if he
thinks it's a corny idea? I'll have to call my bulb
contacts and tell them to cool those bulbs. The Dutch Bulb
Growers is headed by a sweet Dutchman whose name is Harvey
Klahorn. He says "Ya Ya" when things go right and "Oh Oh"
when things go wrong. Try that next time you're in court.

And did you, my dearest, know that breeder bulbs and
their offsets may grow on for years producing only self-
colored flowers, but after a time the progeny break, that
is, produce flowers with the variegation that is so much
prized? Do you think that's what happened to Mama with me?

And what's with you? Mama said you just "picked" at
your lamb. You're such a dear to drop in on the "girls." I
think they miss me. Have you seen the new Truffaut movie? I
think that guy is not too tightly wrapped.

I'm invited to my first official bash. Harold is
throwing a party for Mrs. Montenegro after the press thing.
Did I tell you she pronounces her name "Isa-bey-yah"? I
bet her name was Isabel O'Rourke before she hooked the Duke
of Montenegro. Sorry to go on so about her, but I have that
awful Irish intuition that tells me to be wary.

So take care, my moody black tulip. If you are not
good, I will plunge you into soil and ashes and keep you
in semi-darkness like they do all the bad Darwins. And
then I'll put you in the forcing room until you tell me you
love me.

Your Three Penny Opera

from the chipped chippendale desk of **Penny Smith**

June 23, 1979

To: Sue Ellen Anderson

Tried to catch you for the last three days but your secretary
told me you had to go on a fast trip to Mexico. So I am
resorting to writing down my thoughts for promos before we
hit La Montenegro. I'd turn them in to Harold, but I'm
nervous without trying them out on anyone but my mother who
thinks I'm crazy anyway. Rosemae said she was sending all
your mail to your house this weekend so you'd have a chance
to catch up on everything. So read my letter first.

Plan I. I looked at the rose promo you did a couple of years
ago and TJ tells me it was a big smash. Well, then, why not
another flower? So I sat down and wrote to the consulate of
the Hague and he put me in touch with a nice guy who repre-
sents the tulip growers or bulb snatchers or something.
Anyway, I thought we could do it at the same time the big
festival was on in Holland in the spring. Maybe a "Go Dutch"
theme. I don't know anyone important in the art world but we
could try to get someone famous to draw a tulip for us and
then we could have it printed on different fabrics, etc.
What about the little Dutch shoes? Could kids wear them?
Could we sell them?

        I'm not up on all the resources, but if we had a classy
glass company couldn't they make a tulip-shaped glass for
champagne? And certainly we could do tulip cosmetic tones
and tulip haircuts. Maybe we could get someone to install a
windmill so kids could learn about energy.

Plan II. Instead of the traditional Santa, could we invent a
new character that would be fresh? I thought of Mr. Mistletoe. A Christmas fairy. We could build a gingerbread house
and kids could visit him and get a mistletoe cookie. The
bridal studio is dead at this time of year and Billy Sutton

from the chipped chippendale desk of Penny Smith

says he'd love to set up a gallery where kids would be shot
with the fairy. He would do it with a remote so the kids
wouldn't even know. If we charged, say, $25 for a photo
(which is dirt cheap), don't you think we'd have a minimum of
2,000 kids shot? This is pretty good income--and it could be
a lot more if customers had more than one photo and got one
framed for Grandma.

We could get a lot of publicity mileage out of it as
well as merchandise it. Certainly we could have a mistletoe
wrap. Doesn't the stuff grow wild down here?

Well, that's a beginning anyway. Let me know what you
think. If you like it I'll send it to the great beady-eyed
chief.

from the chipped chippendale desk of **Penny Smith**

From the desk of

Sue Ellen Anderson
Public Relations/Nevins Markham

June 24, 1979

To: Penny Smith

First of all, I'm sorry to be of so little
help on the promotion front, but the
Mexico Fashion Show we're about to throw
is mind-boggling. However, as soon as I
get that off my back I'll help all I can.

As for your ideas, I think they are right
on the button. I love Mr. Mistletoe and I
think Harold will love him. It's a nat-
ural. The tulip thing has a lot of poten-
tial, but you have to be careful to avoid
anything that comes off wooden-shoesy. It
turns the old boy off. Think chic. More
stuff in the Gucci world. Less in the Ya
Ya sabot syndrome. Go ahead and send it.

PLAZA
INTERNATIONAL
HOTEL Canyon Plaza, Canyon City, Texas 78254   311-555-0400

June 25, 1979

Dear Penelope, Penny, Smith, Smithey (What do you like being called?),

I'm so looking forward to meeting you and Sue Ellen Anderson Friday morning. Everything Harold tells me about you makes me feel we'll be a great team. So bring all your problems to me. That's what I'm good for. Best,

Isabella Montenegro

nevins markham

6/25/79

In my latest analysis of missing merchandise in the downtown operation, I
have found that about 80% of it has either <u>been</u> in the advertising department
and has not been returned, or it has been
lost <u>between</u> the display department and
the ad department.

Since I believe this to be a controllable
situation, I am directing the manager of
each department to check all merchandise
in by filling out the attached form and
when merchandise is to be returned, to
get the authorized signature of the
buyer, assistant buyer, or department
manager on the form.

All forms must be sent to me. If anyone
fails to follow this procedure, the
missing items will be charged to the
department the merchandise was last in.

cc: Harold Nevins
      TJ Bennis, Display
      Jean Derujinski, Fashion Office

Nevins Markham Inter-store Transfer Manifest

No. 00100

FROM _____ TO _____ DEPT._____

DATE WRITTEN _____ DATE RECEIVED _____

SENT BY _____ RECEIVED BY _____

BUYER _____ FOR USE BY _____

DIVISION SUPERVISOR _____ DIVISION SUPERVISOR _____

NO. OF ITEM(S) ON LOAN _____

STYLE(S) NO. _____
give complete description of merchandise

KEY REC. OR TRANSFER NO.	DEPT.	NUMBER OF PIECES SENT		RECEIPTS		RECEIVED IN DEPT. & CHECKED BY
		HANGING	BOXED	OVER	SHORT	

DETAIL	DEPT.	RETAIL	EXPLANATION _____
			4-PART FORM USE BALL POINT & BEAR DOWN

June 27, 1979

to: TJ Bennis

I cannot be available during the mornings any
longer. I will be filling out Carl Jurken-
Spitz's security forms. Is there some way
Display could get the stuff directly from
departments and not have merch. sent up here
first? As it is we get about 150 different
pieces of merchandise each week. With your
window stuff it climbs to well above 250, and I
don't even want to think of interior displays.
If Rosemae, our secretary, fills out all the
forms, she has no time to type any letters or
copy and god forbid the artist should fill out
anything so mundane. So I'd really appreciate it
if your kids would do Display stuff and I'll do
Advertising stuff.

from the chipped chippendale desk of Penny Smith

June 28, 1979

Ms. Isabella Montenegro
Plaza International Hotel
Suite 2100
Canyon Plaza
Canyon City, Texas 78254

Welcome!

I too look forward to our meeting
tomorrow. Sue Ellen and I will be there
at 10 as you requested. I'll have all the
stuff on Christmas. I have a super idea.
Also some goodies for spring. As for what
I like to be called, I just remember what
my mother always says, "I don't care what
you call me, as long as you don't call me
late for dinner." See ya.

Penelope Smith

hand deliver
with bouquet of
yellow tulips

from the chipped chippendale desk of Penny Smith

Saturday Black Saturday

Dear Dar,

My gut feeling was right on target re Mrs.
Montenegro. Just read the clip from this morning's paper. Met her yesterday. She swept into
the room like she was the Holy Father and we were
an audience of two from Muscatine, Iowa.

"Tell me all," she cooed. And we did. We
spilled the Mistletoe Fairy. We spilled the
tulips. We spilled Mexico. She picked at her
eggs but she ate our words (obviously).

But let me tell you--she's quite a looker.
A cross between Mrs. Pynchon on "Lou Grant" and
Faye Dunaway. She was wearing a Geoffrey Beene
beige chiffon. She looked smashing.

Sue Ellen and I are going to drink tonight
to see if we can figure out her angles. I sure
wish I looked like Margaux Hemingway instead of
Gilda Radner. Despairingly,
                    the battered Penny

from the chipped chippendale desk of Penny Smith

NEW YORKER JOINS NEVINS MARKHAM

Author and Promoter Takes Ad Position

By ERNESTINE GUNN

CANYON CITY, Texas, June 30 — Yesterday Nevins Markham introduced Mrs. Isabella Montenegro, newly appointed Vice-President of Sales Promotion for the store.

Mrs. Montenegro, accompanied by a brace of cream-colored Salukis wearing pale yellow leads, unfolded to town leaders her plans for some novel promotions at Nevins Markham.

"Even though it's early and might seem premature to people to be talking about Christmas," she observed, "one must always remember that Christmas comes in June to a store. The delicious thing I'm planning right now is not a 'Santy Claus'— other stores can have him. I'm going to have a Mr. Mistletoe. It's a whole new concept for children for Christmas. I plan to talk to Maurice Sendak about doing a new fairy-tale book just for us, and I would just love to see what Angelo Donghia would do with a gingerbread house.

"Come spring, I am thinking one word—tulip. But I can't say more!"

When asked whether or not she had a nickname, Mrs. Montenegro wittily replied, "You can call me anything, but don't call me late for dinner. That's what my mama always said."

Mrs. Montenegro hails from New York, where she was head of publicity for Seven Arts Studio. She is the author of the best-selling novel *Chic to Chic.* Mrs. Montenegro also raises Salukis at her country home on Long Island.

New Address for
Penelope Smith
687 Shinstone
Canyon City, Texas 78251
Phone: (311) 555-2307
Cable: Smith-stone

nevins markham

to: Sue Ellen Anderson, Penelope Smith,
TJ Bennis, Jean Derujinski

from: Harold Nevins

July 2, 1979

Since Mrs. Montenegro will be busy the
first few weeks moving and trying to get
organized, I would like to have your
thoughts on how we might implement her
very splendid ideas for Christmas and
spring. Let's set up a meeting for
Thursday, July 5, at 10 A.M.

HN/bb

July 4

Happy Fourth, Mama! Today is moving day for me.
I sent out a card to all my pals and to you and
Gran and Aunt Amey announcing my new abode and
phone number. But I'll probably call you tonight
anyway. I'm homesick. But I've also been working
very hard. I met the new v.p. sales promotion
lady and she's very good-looking. It will take
me awhile to get to know her. The little studio
apartment I took is very nice. All furnished so
I don't have to sink my bucks into furniture.
Not yet anyway. I've been to a party at Mr.
Nevins's house. What a pad! Very contemporary
with great paintings and lots of gallery
lighting.

The people who rented me my place are very nice.
She's a night nurse and he's a fireman. They
have a little girl about 12 who is almost 5'10".
Tall, lanky, lean Texan type. Her name is Willie
Pearl. She has a jet-black dog that she calls
Spot. I asked her how come "Spot" for a jet-
black dog and she said, "Ah jes lak that name."
Anyway, I think this will do quite nicely for
the time being, and I promise you I'll get
plenty of ferns. Have a nice holiday and give my
love to AA and Gran. Love,

Penny

from the chipped chippendale desk of Penny Smith

July 5

to: Sue Ellen

from: The ex-Mrs. Mistletoe

Here's a list of loonies the Canyon City
Repertory Theatre gave me for possible Mr.
Mistletoes. Of course, you know where I'd like
to shove it at this point. Do you want to pick
someone, or should we let Isabeyyah have all the
fun? Is there anything we can do--like putting
out a contract on her?

Independence Day

Dear Penelope,

Well, we just finished our 4th of July dinner, and
Aunt Amey and Gran wanted to go home before any fireworks
started. We had corn on the cob, chicken, and lemon pie.
Real good American dinner. Amey was gung-ho to bring a ham
for the dinner on discount, but Field's didn't have the
Krakus Atalantis brand--so, no ham. Amey is just bugs on
Polish ham. I can't tell the difference.

Needless to say, we were all in a state of shock with
the picture of your new home. Gran wonders who on earth
will do the windows. I thought the cow must be a joke, but
Gran says indeed not, cows walk in the streets of Texas
just like in India.

I've been trying to get some cartons from the A&P to
send your books in. I've got them all dusted. I must say
you are certainly an expert on filth. The Sisters at
Excelsior would be amazed at your literary taste. Faulkner
and Miller and Joyce. All trash. I can understand Faulkner
as he was a southerner and they all tend to have dirty
minds. Aunt Amey says you should treat yourself to Victoria
Holt. She tells a good story with none of that sex stuff.

I asked Darwin to come for ham but he was out of town.
Just as well, as we ended up with chicken. He said you were
having trouble already with your new boss. Take my advice.
Have respect for your employers.

I know you'll be glad to get your things and get
settled. Certainly a hotel is no place to live, but they do
have a Bible in each room and that's more than you have in
your book collection. Love,

Mother

July 5

Hey Penny! Where's your sense of humor? Stop fretting. You
know there are more criminals outside jails than in. Sure
there is nothing more maddening than having your own idea
swiped. Obviﾎously xxxxxxxxxxx the lady is not as smart about
stores as she'd like the worﾉld to think.ﾐ Sooo any idea that
flys by she is going to grab till she establiﾎhes a beach-
heaﾐd. But you got to take a bigger view of the whole
situaﾉtion. The xﾐﾎxxxxx reason you are in Caﾐyon City and not
playing with mﾉie here is that you want tooﾐ get to learn
retailing from the top bananas. The pros. Righht? So forget
your ego and your sense of fﾐairplaﾐy. She'll find other brains
to pick. Youﾐ're half her age.You'll get there.Kﾎﾎﾐ all your
stuff in writing.Start a dosier. Send copies to anyone you can
find. It will drive her up the wall but it will cover you. She
thinks you are a naive.She thinks you are a rube/ Let her
think so. She'll get lazy and you can put the skrews in her. As
your Aunt Amey says, "give her enough rope and she'll banﾐ
herself with it."

Anyway, Penny, don't worry anymore. Iwish I were there to
shoreyou up. I haﾐ to go. I'm takﾐng Mr. Sharpless and wifey
to see Annie tonight. Mrs.Sharpless doesnt hear and he doesn't
see. Hopeﾐ Sandy barks alot. I'll be away this weekend. I'll
call you. If things get too tough rememxxxber that you can
always wrap it up, take over my apartment, my cat and my
laundry. Even if we had to exchange slave bracelts at some
bizaare church service to please your Ma I'd do it. Love you
dearlyenough for me to have typed thismyself. Dar

ps. your ma called and said you are living with a
nurse?????????

Canyon City Bank
PERSONAL LOAN APPLICATION

I hereby make application for $ __5,000__ for __36__ months for ☒ Auto ☐ Property Improvement

☐ Other _____ Send Mail to: ☒ Home ☐ Business

1. TELL US ABOUT YOURSELF

(Title Optional) ☐ Mr. ☐ Mrs. ☐ Miss ☒ Ms.

Full Name (please print) First	Middle	Last	Social Security Number
Penelope		Smith	3 2 3 1 4 2 1 6 6

Present Home Address — Number and Street	Apt. No.	City	State	Zip Code	Years There
687 Shinstone		Canyon City	Tex.	78251	1 mo.

Area Code Home Phone		Monthly Rent/Mtge.	Date of Birth	No. of Dependents (include self)	List Automobiles Owned Year / Make
(311) 555-2307	☐ Own ☒ Rent	$233.00	11/19/56	0	xxxxxxxxxxxxxxxx

Previous Home Address — Number and Street	City	State	Zip Code	Years There
8518 W. Winston Dr.	Chicago	Ill.	60611	23

2. TELL US ABOUT YOUR INCOME

Present Employer or Business — Name	Check Only If: Owner	Partner	Officer
Nevins Markham	☐	☐	☐

Business Address — Number and Street	City	State	Zip Code	Years There
Elm & Orchard	Canyon City	Tex.	78254	1 mo.

Area Code Business Phone	Position	Dept. Name/No.	Employee/Badge No.	Annual Income
(311) 555-0500	Advertising Mgr.			$15,000

Previous Employer or Business — Name		Position
Carson Pirie Scott & Co.		Copy Chief

Business Address — Number and Street	City	State	Zip Code	Years There
State & Monroe	Chicago	Ill.	60603	2

OTHER INCOME (Note: Indicate pensions, public assistance program, dividends and annuities, etc. Provide full details below—attach separate sheet if necessary. Please do not indicate income from alimony, child support or separate maintenance payments unless you wish us to consider this income during our review of your application.)

AMOUNT $ __000.00__ SOURCE _____

3. TELL US ABOUT YOUR CREDIT REFERENCES

(Please indicate if the name on the account is different than the one you have used on this application.)

	Bank Name and Address	Account Number
Savings Account	First National Bank Chicago	07104037642
Personal Checking Account	Canyon City Bank	0555116-1
Business Checking Account		

List below all outstanding indebtedness. Include credit cards. Attach a separate sheet if necessary (if none write none)

Creditor/Mortgage Holder Name and Address	Account Number	Original Amount	Balance	Monthly Payments
American Express	371871863	$150.87	$100.87	$50
Carson Pirie Scott & Co.	350 332 48	85.00	35.00	35

Name and Address of nearest relative not living with you		Relationship
Mrs. Daisy M. Smith 8518 W. Winston Dr., Chicago		Mother

Have you ever applied to this Bank for a Personal Loan, Master Charge, Visa or Overdraft Account? ☐ Yes ☒ No   If yes list current Account Numbers __xxxxxxxxxxxxxxx__

4. OTHER INFORMATION

I have completely and correctly answered all the questions on this application.

During the review of my application the bank may obtain a consumer report on me and if the application is approved the bank may at any time in the future obtain additional consumer reports to review my account. I have the right to ask for the name and address of the consumer reporting agency which gave the bank the consumer report.

Applicant Sign Here X _Penelope Smith_ (Full Signature)   Date __7/5/79__

SPACE RESERVED FOR BANK USE ONLY

Approval		Employee No.	CL $	No. CDS

Date	H$	P	D	W	P	D	W

NO	AMT	BAL	LC	1ST	2ND	ST	CM NO	AMT	BAL	LC	1ST	2ND	ST

Issued	C.L.	Bal.	D.L.P.	Amt.	Exp. Date	Acct. Stat.	Del. Cycle

Member FDIC

Isabella Montenegro

Vice-President/Nevins Markham
Sales Promotion

July 9, 1979

To: TJ Bennis, Display

When can I see sketches of my Mistletoe
Fairy's house? I am hungry for them. I
see something gingerbready. Hope you do,
too.

cc: Harold Nevins

IM/rm

nevins markham

July 10, 1979

Sorry I haven't had a minute to even think about
Christmas since I bought decorations and fixtures
last May. After 14 Christmases I have found that no
matter how you slice it, fall comes first. However,
I'll try to get something down on paper for the
fairy's shelter. I think gingerbready is wrong for
our store. I think it should have a slick Christmas
freshness to it. Perhaps we could construct a fern
house with lots of mistletoe tied into it. After
all, it does grow wild in Texas. Chances are someone
will want to buy it for their garden, so it might as
well be something expensive. We sold stuff like this
every year and we can often turn a good profit on a
display.

cc: Penelope Smith
    Sue Ellen Anderson
    Jean Derujinski

Isabella Montenegro

Vice-President/Nevins Markham
Sales Promotion

July 11, 1979

To: Jean Derujinski, Fashion Dept.

How is my Mr. Mistletoe's costume coming?
When can I see sketches of it? I see
something very ferny and green with lots
of mistletoe strung on it. After all, it
grows wild here so we might as well take
advantage of nature's goodness. Ms.
Bennis thinks "gingerbready" but that's
much too Hansel and Gretel-y for my
taste. Keep it more "Puck," more
"Ariel." Since I understand we often
sell things we have made, it might as
well be a production number. That way we
can make a handsome profit on it.

cc: Harold Nevins

IM/rm

July 12

to: Sue Ellen

Just happened to see this bill in the
production department. I could be out of
my tree, but I thought those Salukis
belonged to the famous breeder of dis-
content--our very own Mrs. Montenegro. Do
you think it would be out of line to get a
copy into circulation?

CANYON CITY KENNELS 109 Rio Seco Drive, Canyon City, Texas 78254

"no bark, no bite"

Mrs. Isabella Montenegro
Sales Promotion Director
Nevins Markham
Elm and Orchard
Canyon City, Texas 78254

INVOICE 30175

ORDER NO. 71

DEPT.

SALESMAN

DATE 7/10/79

DELIVERY Plaza Inter-
national Hotel

SHIPPING DATE pick up--same

TERMS: NET 30

QUANTITY	DESCRIPTION	AMOUNT		TOTAL	
	Rental of Salukis Mai & Tai for publicity and photography			$150	00
	taxis			10	00
				$160	00

RECEIVED JUL 11 1979

July 12, 1979

To: Sue Ellen Anderson

I have just hired Frederico Lilac, ballet
dancer, to be my Mr. Mistletoe. He is
with the Monaco Ballet and he's agreed
to play the role of Mr. Mistletoe as a
special favor to me. (Besides, it will be
great publicity for him.)

Mr. Nevins told me that you had already
queried Time about doing a little squib
in the "People, Places" column. In the
future, please let me know before you
query anyone. I have all sorts of great
contacts and connections and could most
certainly put you in the right hands. As
a matter of fact, I think that I should
see all releases before they go out so
that I can make some contributions.

cc: Harold Nevins

IM/rm

nevins markham

to: TJ Bennis

from: Harold Nevins

July 12, 1979

What's happening on the mistletoe house? Mrs.
Montenegro wants to do some publicity and needs to
see sketches desperately. Just drop everything else
for the moment and get on this project. She has
something lined up with <u>Time</u> and I don't want to
miss out on it.

cc: Isabella Montenegro

HN/bb

Isabella Montenegro

Vice-President/Nevins Markham
Sales Promotion

July 13, 1979

To: Sue Ellen Anderson
    Penelope Smith

From now on I don't think it will be necessary for either of you to take your valuable time to attend promotion meetings with the buyers and merchandise people. I think the simpler we make these things the more creative we can be. I'll do all the hard legwork up front, and I'm counting on you people to worry out the mechanics.

Please see that you have a detailed weekly plan on my desk each Monday at 9:30, with monthly outlines of forthcoming promotions and their current status. Then I can coordinate them and make everything go more smoothly.

IM/rm

Texas Store Buys All New Sablinka Skins at NY Auction

Pays Top Price

July 16 (AP) — Hannah Nevins, Executive Vice-President and member of the Board of the famous Texas store Nevins Markham, stopped the St. Lawrence Fur Auction yesterday when she out bid all participants for all the "Sablinka" skins, a new soft gray fur which is a cross between Russian sable and U.S. blue mutation mink.

Howard Silvers, breeder and owner of the Rajah Mink Ranch, in Utah, has been working to achieve this particular cross for over 15 years. Until now, no fur breeder has been able to get a breeder sable out of Russia alive. Mr. Silvers's story reads like a Len Deighton spy caper. Silvers bought his Russian male sables through an intermediary breeder from Yugoslavia who smuggled them into Sweden. The Rajah Breeder Association then set up a breeding farm in Fjordlo and introduced the Russian sables to the mutation minks from America. "If you think making a Russian sable fall in love with an American mink is easy, you're dead wrong. It took us 13 years of coaxing to achieve one love affair."

Ms. Nevins, glowing with pride after the auction, said, "The Sablinkas are rare and beautiful and worth every cent I bid for them." (She paid $1,000 for each female pelt and $800 for each male.) "At least 100 of our customers will want this one coat. I'm having Pauline Trigère design the coat because she is the one American designer who understands both coats and furs. She is the only one I would trust with my Sablinkas."

Nevins Markham expects the coat to retail for about $100,000, which is just a drop in the bucket for a store located deep in oil land.

The Sablinka by Trigère will be presented at the Nevins Markham Fashion Gala in September in Canyon City.

nevins markham

July 18, 1979

To: Harold Nevins

From: Isabella Montenegro

I want to pull out all stops
on Ms. Hannah's buy of the
Sablinkas. I called Howie
Silvers (an old flame of mine)
and he's willing to run this ad
on page 2 of next Sunday's New
York Times. I just want to
check it out with you. I'm
confident that Ms. Hannah will
be pleased to get this kind of
recognition for her glorious
taste, and it won't hurt our
little ole reputation none. I'm
just thrilled.

IM/rm

Canyon City Bank
(the bank that's like a father to you!)

July 27, 1979

Ms. Penelope Smith
687 Shinstone
Canyon City, Texas 78251

Dear Ms. Smith,

We have received your application
for a car loan and have reviewed it.
Although we appreciate your business, our
loan committee feels that you have not
worked in the Canyon City area long
enough to show job longevity. We hope you
will continue to do business with us and
that we can be of help to you at another
time.

Sincerely yours,

L. B. Ross
Loan Officer

nevins markham

elm and orchard
canyon city, texas 78254

July 30, 1979

Mr. John H. Farrell, Jr.
President
Canyon City Bank
Canyon Plaza
Canyon City, Tex. 78254

Dear Mr. Farrell,

Recently I took one of your advertisements seriously.
It showed a young working woman (attaché case et al.)
buying a car. The headline of this full-page ad read,
"When a working woman wants a car, we'll drive her to the
dealer." The ad was signed "Canyon City Bank--the bank
that's like a father to you."

"Well, now," I said, "I'm a working woman and my
salary is good. (For a woman, that is.) I have worked at
Nevins Markham in the capacity of Advertising Manager
since June 2, 1979. Prior to that, I worked at Carson Pirie
Scott & Co. in Chicago for two years. Before that, I
attended the U. of Wisconsin Graduate School and worked in
the library there. In fact, I have worked every day since I
got out of high school. So I feel my record is very good.

However, when I applied for a car loan, the bank
that's like a father to me treated me like an orphan. I was
turned down on the basis of job longevity. It is hard for
me to think of a way I could have more longev.

I think your ad is misleading and downright
untruthful. If you have to earn a certain salary, say so.
If you have to be a Canyon City resident for five years
before you qualify, say so in your ad. I need a car. I have
the down payment. I can afford the monthly payments. So
what's up, father?

Sincerely yours,

Penelope Smith
Advertising Manager

nevins markham
elm and orchard
canyon city, texas 78254

July 31, 1979

Ms. Carol Channing
Theatre Royal
Drury Lane
Catherine Street
London W1, England

Dear Ms. Channing,

As you probably read, Nevins Markham has purchased
all the Sablinka skins in the world. (In case you did miss
this world-shaking news, Sablinka is the first cross-bred
fur in the world, accomplished by mating a Russian sable
with an American mutation mink!)

I would love to advertise the mink on someone famous.
A kind of "What Becomes a Legend Most" but more fun than
that. We have a super artist here who has taken the liberty
of drawing you with the proposed coat. I'm sending you a
photostat of it so that you can see it. I would like to use
the drawing in an ad and in blow-ups for the main window.
I'd love to have a radio commercial done, but with you
being so many miles away this might be tricky.

Naturally you have probably guessed what I have in
mind for the heading. Right. "Sablinkas are a girl's best
friend." If you agree, I'll get the rights to the music.

Now comes the inevitable agent's query. What's in it
for Carol? Just super PR, Ms. Channing, and Mr. Nevins says
you can have anything you like out of our Christmas
catalogue. Mr. Nevins also sends his best to you. If it's
OK, will you sign the attached release? Have a happy
Sablinka.

Best,

Penelope Smith
Advertising Manager

enc: photostat of drawing
PS/ps

nevins markham

8/1/79

I assume that Ms. Smith has brought you up to date
on the various systems we have for returning all
merchandise to the proper departments after it has
been signed out to Advertising and Display and
Fashion Shows. This is an enormously important
process whereby the Security Department can keep
tabs on merchandise. As you know, about 90% of all
shoplifting is done by in-house personnel. In the
past month I have kept track of Advertising sign-
outs and returns. Several hundred dollars' worth of
goods that were borrowed during the first part of
July have remained open on the books. I have checked
with Ms'. Smith, and she says she has no record of
this merchandise other than that it was returned by
store messenger. Although I had warned her
repeatedly that checking merchandise back into the
departments with proper procedure was vital, she
has not done so. Now that you are in charge of Sales
Promotion and can have some control over Display,
Fashion, and Advertising, I am sure you will do
whatever you can to police this. (Incidentally, I
was very impressed with the article on you in the
newspaper.) Thanks.

Isabella Montenegro

Vice-President/Nevins Markham
Sales Promotion

August 2, 1979

To: Penelope Smith
    Sue Ellen Anderson
    TJ Bennis
    Jean Derujinski

I'm enclosing Carl Jurgen-Spitz's memo regarding the handling of merchandise in your departments and the amount of merchandise that just <u>seems</u> to be missing. I cannot allow this kind of sloppy organization to continue. I want a memo from each one of you giving full details of what you now have in your various departments, when you expect to return it, and how you expect to have it returned. And I want it today. This cannot (and underline the cannot) go on.

cc: Harold Nevins
    Carl Jurgen-Spitz

IM/rm

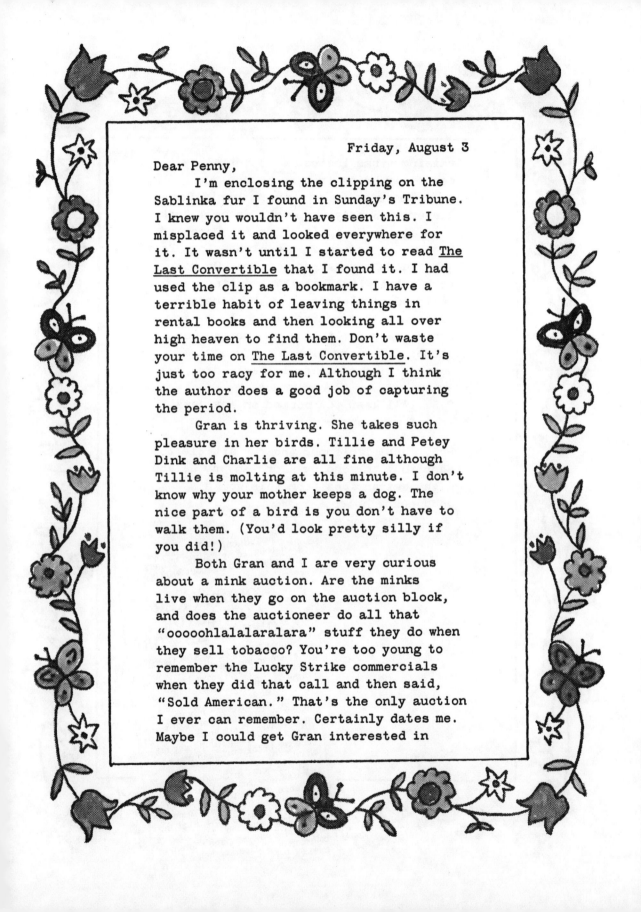

Friday, August 3

Dear Penny,

    I'm enclosing the clipping on the
Sablinka fur I found in Sunday's Tribune.
I knew you wouldn't have seen this. I
misplaced it and looked everywhere for
it. It wasn't until I started to read <u>The
Last Convertible</u> that I found it. I had
used the clip as a bookmark. I have a
terrible habit of leaving things in
rental books and then looking all over
high heaven to find them. Don't waste
your time on <u>The Last Convertible</u>. It's
just too racy for me. Although I think
the author does a good job of capturing
the period.

    Gran is thriving. She takes such
pleasure in her birds. Tillie and Petey
Dink and Charlie are all fine although
Tillie is molting at this minute. I don't
know why your mother keeps a dog. The
nice part of a bird is you don't have to
walk them. (You'd look pretty silly if
you did!)

    Both Gran and I are very curious
about a mink auction. Are the minks
live when they go on the auction block,
and does the auctioneer do all that
"ooooohlalalaralara" stuff they do when
they sell tobacco? You're too young to
remember the Lucky Strike commercials
when they did that call and then said,
"Sold American." That's the only auction
I ever can remember. Certainly dates me.
Maybe I could get Gran interested in

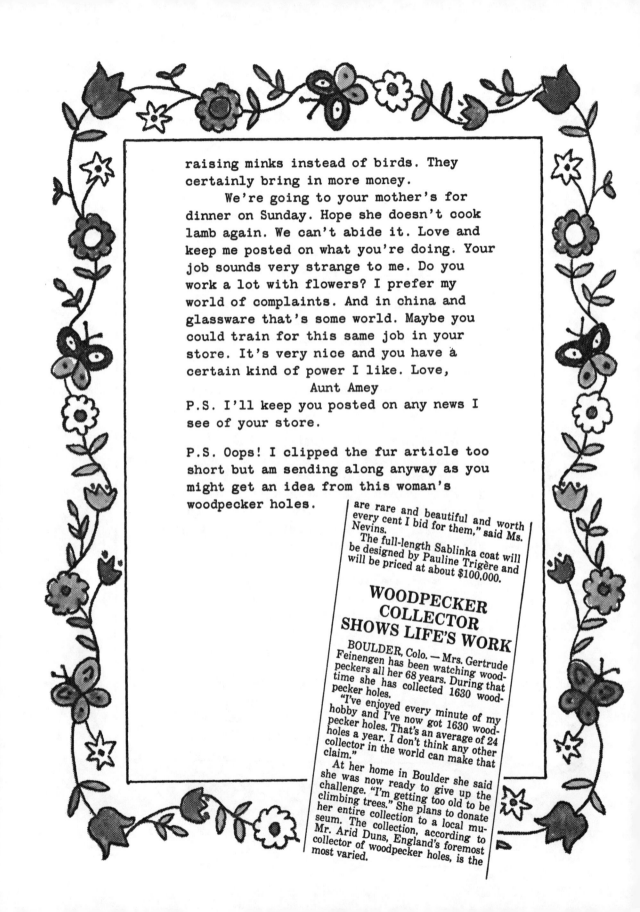

raising minks instead of birds. They
certainly bring in more money.

We're going to your mother's for
dinner on Sunday. Hope she doesn't cook
lamb again. We can't abide it. Love and
keep me posted on what you're doing. Your
job sounds very strange to me. Do you
work a lot with flowers? I prefer my
world of complaints. And in china and
glassware that's some world. Maybe you
could train for this same job in your
store. It's very nice and you have a
certain kind of power I like. Love,
                    Aunt Amey
P.S. I'll keep you posted on any news I
see of your store.

P.S. Oops! I clipped the fur article too
short but am sending along anyway as you
might get an idea from this woman's
woodpecker holes.

are rare and beautiful and worth
every cent I bid for them," said Ms.
Nevins.

The full-length Sablinka coat will
be designed by Pauline Trigère and
will be priced at about $100,000.

WOODPECKER COLLECTOR SHOWS LIFE'S WORK

BOULDER, Colo. — Mrs. Gertrude
Feinengen has been watching wood-
peckers all her 68 years. During that
time she has collected 1630 woodpecker holes.

"I've enjoyed every minute of my
hobby and I've now got 1630 woodpecker holes. That's an average of 24
holes a year. I don't think any other
collector in the world can make that
claim."

At her home in Boulder she said
she was now ready to give up the
challenge. "I'm getting too old to be
climbing trees." She plans to donate
her entire collection to a local museum. The collection, according to
Mr. Arid Duns, England's foremost
collector of woodpecker holes, is the
most varied.

nevins markham

8/7/79

I am requesting permission to spend time with Penny
Smith in the Ad Department. It can be when you think
she isn't busy on her regular work. I feel that if I
can show her the forms and explain how to fill them
out completely she might get the hang of it.

Isabella Montenegro

Vice-President/Nevins Markham
Sales Promotion

August 8, 1979

Smithey:

Your gold sale sounds like the <u>Wall
Street Journal</u> six o'clock round-up.
Don't you think you could put some punch
in this? Some urgency. Give it some
balls, baby. Or don't you know about
balls, baby?

IM/rm

Isabella Montenegro

Vice-President/Nevins Markham
Sales Promotion

August 8, 1979

To: Penny Smith
    Bill Lance

I think it would be a wise procedure if no
advertisement is released in the future
without my sig on it. Once I have signed
it, no further changes are to be made. If
I'm out of reach, Smithey can call it in.

IM/rm

Aug. 9

to: Isabella Montenegro

OK. I thought the commodity market and
gold prices were a hook. So did the
buyer. However, I've given some alter-
native headlines to Bill Lance. Bounce
them around and choose whichever ball
pleases you most. I'll be with Tiny
Halmark in the coat dept. working on her
August coat special.

Isabella Montenegro

Vice-President/Nevins Markham
Sales Promotion

August 10, 1979

To: Bill Lance

Please see that the following headline is set up on
the Sunday gold ad. I want it big and I want it
gutsy and I want it read. Bold Bold Bold. The rest
of the copy is OK. Smith's versions were milky.

SENSATIONAL! SENSATIONAL! SENSATIONAL!
GOLD PAVILION REDUCES GOLD PRICES!
NEVINS MARKHAM GRABS UP THE LOT!
INCREDIBLE PRICES ON 14K AND 18K JEWELRY.
SAVE BIG MONEY ON SOARING COMMODITY!
SENSATIONAL!

IM/rm

From the desk of

Sue Ellen Anderson
Public Relations/Nevins Markham

August 15, 1979

To: Isabella Montenegro

I understand completely that you want
to pull out all stops on the Sablinka
promotion. Will you approve an extra two
grand to cinch the "Merv Griffin Show"?
He will give us an entire segment with
either Hannah Nevins or Howie Silvers or
both, but we'll have to provide models
and pay their fares out to the coast. I'm
also working on "60 Minutes" and there
will be expenses on that. Sablinka was a
surprise and one that shocked my budget.
Please advise.

cc: Harold Nevins

nevins markham

inter-office memo

to: Isabella Montenegro

from: Hannah Nevins

August 16, 1979

I was shocked and dismayed to see last Sunday's ad
on the gold sale. No less than four "sensationals"
were used. This seems like we have on our payroll a
writer with a very limited vocabulary. Besides
that, I have somehow always managed to reserve the
word "sensational" for the Immaculate Conception.

cc: Harold Nevins

HN/ub

Isabella Montenegro

Vice-President/Nevins Markham
Sales Promotion

August 17, 1979

To: Penelope Smith
    Sue Ellen Anderson
    TJ Bennis
    Jean Derujinski

I'm sending along Ms. Hannah's comments
on the Sunday gold sale advertisement
regarding the use of the word
"sensational." I think she has a good
point. It does not make us sound like a
fine store. Please refrain from ever
using this word in the future in an ad, a
window card, an interior design card, a
statement enclosure, a TV commercial, a
radio commercial, a press release, or any
form of communication in the store. In
other words, let me spell it out loud and
clear. The word "sensational" is taboo
at Nevins Markham.

cc: Hannah Nevins
    Harold Nevins

IM/rm

Isabella Montenegro

Vice-President/Nevins Markham
Sales Promotion

August 20, 1979

To: Sue Ellen Anderson

It has always seemed to me that Public
Relations and Publicity were in the
"freebie" department. We spend plenty of
dollars in advertising. I think we ought
to get our PR without costs. I'll take
the ropes on in finagling the dollars out
of Merv and "60 Minutes." Either we are
interesting enough for them to cover or
we are not--or perhaps we're not getting
across.

cc: Harold Nevins

IM/rm

Aug. 21

to: Sue Ellen Anderson
    TJ Bennis
    Jean Derujinski
    Bill Lance
    Stella Branden

re: the complete promotion plans for the
    destruction of Isabella Montenegro

The PR department and the ad department are offering
a prize for the best plan to destruct Mrs. Isabeyyah
Montenegro. My suggestions below; others are
welcome.

1. Quick stabs to the heart. Plan would be
   appropriate for St. Valentine's Day
   promotion.

2. Drawing and quartering her in employees'
   cafeteria kitchen.

3. Pulling out nails (finger and toe) in beauty
   salon.

4. Covering her with hot wax and placing her in
   main window under our very own sensational
   Sablinka (with or without Howie Silvers).

5. Released to local press to have their way
   with her.

6. Chained to a rubber fireplug in the doggy
   department.

All entries must be in by Dec. 1, 1979. Only
employees and their families are eligible to
compete.

from the chipped chippendale desk of **Penny Smith**

Isabella Montenegro

Vice-President/Nevins Markham
Sales Promotion

August 24, 1979

To: Harold Nevins
    Penelope Smith
    TJ Bennis

Just want to bring you up to date on the many splendored plans
we now have going on our Sablinka promo.

ADVERTISING   I think we've copped a winner with Carol
Channing. She's agreed to let us sketch her
wearing it. It's a winner.

PR   As you know, I've got Merv and "60 Minutes" and
I'm talking to "Good Morning America," Tom
Snyder, Rona Barrett, "Today," etc.

We're all set in <u>Vogue</u>, <u>Bazaar</u>, <u>W</u>, and <u>Town and
Country</u>. Sue Ellen is on top of the local stuff.
We may have to pick up a couple of tabs for
travel. It's probably worth it.

DISPLAY   Beginning the first week in December the big
window will be completely darkened--all you'll
see is a huge Mosler safe with pelts hanging out
of it. Should be most effective. TJ thought she
could do something with an alarm that would be
triggered if the window is touched. I don't
know. I like her idea of roping off the window,
but alarms . . . ? Nice thing about this is that
the coat stays on the floor where it has a
chance of being sold.

TRUCKS, ETC.   We have poster permission from Channing and I'm
going to have them slapped up on our delivery
trucks and warehouse signs.

FASHION SHOWS   Sablinka will be in five major fashion shows as
the finale. I'll have Derujinski give you a
schedule so you'll know when the coat is in the
store or out of the store. I think we're on our
way!

IM/rm

Aug. 27, 1979

to: Sue Ellen Anderson
    M. Farrar, Legal
    Isabella Montenegro

I just want to go on record that
Channing's agreement with us was for
one radio spot to be played in this
market only. One ad to be run full-page
in both papers and a poster which she may
or may not autograph. But we have no
permission to put her on trucks or
warehouse posters and I have no com-
mitment that she would appear on the
Griffin show wearing it. Also, no one
thought it out that she might order the
Great Wall from the catalogue.

from the chipped chippendale desk of Penny Smith

nevins markham

to: Isabella Montenegro

from: Hannah Nevins

September 4, 1979

It seems odd to me that, although Nevins Markham
sells more fine furs than anyone else in the
Southwest, we have a singularly poor record of
storage and remodeling. I think it's just plain
lack of promotion on the part of the store and a
lackluster attitude we all take toward departments
such as these.

Granted, they are not the high-glamour areas. But
they can be high-profit centers. And the profit is
in remodeling. Once you get a fur in for storage, a
woman can be conned into doing something with it.

If you relate the time of the executive body of
merchandise people and buyers and top salespeople
(to whom we pay a fat commission on furs) to the
time and energy it takes to promote storage and
remodeling where no executive energy is used, you
can see how valuable a business like this can be to
Nevins Markham.

You've been so very good in coming up with plans for
exciting promotions, I am turning this over to you
to see what you can come up with. Just turn on those
creative juices that made Mr. Mistletoe and we'll
have it made.

HN/ub

Isabella Montenegro

Vice-President/Nevins Markham
Sales Promotion

September 5, 1979

To: Smithey

I think we should come up with a slogan
for Sablinka. How do you like "Ours alone
in the world"? Also, I'd like to get a
major plan going on fur storage. Get Sue
Ellen and the kids together and make a
master plan of it. I really haven't the
time to play with this as I'm just snowed
with Channing and Frederico's costume,
etc. You ought to be able to swing with
this one all on your own.

IM/rm

Sept. 7

to: Isabella Montenegro

"Ours alone in the world" is a very good
slogan. I imagine Lord & Taylor thought
so too when they coined it many years
ago. I always thought they should have
tagged onto it "because no one else will
buy it."

As for the fur storage problem, I'll be
happy to swing on this "alone." But who
has materials? What's the budget? And
what do we do with storage and remodeling
that no one else in the world does? Got
some thoughts or do I have permission to
venture out of my office into the
glamorous world of Hannah Nevins?

from the chipped chippendale desk of Penny Smith

Isabella Montenegro

Vice-President/Nevins Markham
Sales Promotion

September 10, 1979

To: Smithey

When I talked to Carol Channing the other night in London, I told her I'd taken a wee bit of license. So she said, "Great. I'll just take a wee bit of license with my Christmas catalogue list." Now take a tip from me, Ms. Smith. If you had sewed up this deal properly at the very beginning, we wouldn't be phoning up for every little thing we now need. Also, did you tell her she could order "anything" from the catalogue? That could get plenty expensive. In the future, let's try to get the act together and avoid all legal hassles.

cc: H. Nevins
    M. Farrar, Legal

IM/rm

nevins markham

September 14, 1979

I've convinced Charles Chipmonk, Chief of the Utes
in New Mexico, to come to the store for an exhibit
of his sand paintings. I arranged for him to be here
early in the year. This is a time when it's dull as
dishwater in the store and we need extra promotional
push besides after-Christmas sales.

Chipmonk is a very civilized and talented man. He's
a University of New Mexico graduate, and his work
has been shown in just about every good museum in
the world. He lives in Santa Fe, or I guess I should
say he lives it up in Santa Fe. I know you'll enjoy
him. Our dates simply didn't mesh (he's available
January 10-11), but Hannah will be happy to host a
party for him at the Jacaranda Club. I think we
should have a couple of hundred of our antiques/fine
arts customers, and Sue Ellen will help build a
press list for you. I'm going to unload a couple of
my Chipmonk paintings after he goes, and this will
help get the price up.

cc: Hannah Nevins

HN/bb

Isabella Montenegro

Vice-President/Nevins Markham
Sales Promotion

September 17, 1979

To: Sue Ellen Anderson
    TJ Bennis
    Penelope Smith
    Jean Derujinski

Mr. Nevins has arranged for Charles
Chipmonk to show his sand paintings on
January 10-11. Neither Mr. Nevins nor I
will be in town at that time. I'll be on a
swing to Switzerland to see if I can tie
up our doing Swissair uniforms, and Mr.
Nevins will be in New York with the
buyers. Therefore I'm turning over the
project to Smith and Anderson. Give me
all plans before you finalize them. Thank
you.

cc: Harold Nevins
    Hannah Nevins

IM/rm

Isabella Montenegro

Vice-President/Nevins Markham
Sales Promotion

Confidential

September 17, 1979

To: Harold Nevins

I don't want to say anything about Sue
Ellen's problem, but I'd like to know
just how to cope with it. As you know, at
the Republic National Bank Fashion Show
she threw hard rolls at Carl Jurgen-
Spitz. Got some of your good advice for
little ole me?

nevins markham

inter-office memo

to: Isabella Montenegro

from: Harold Nevins

Confidential

September 21, 1979

I'll talk to Sue Ellen. She does from
time to time have a drink too many, but
she has always controlled it in the past
and she does do a good job with the
locals. I guess my advice is patience
with a dash of impatience.

nevins markham

September 24, 1979

I'm sending along a little note that I want to get
out to the "Triple A's" right away. I want it to go
on my personal stationery.

Since you are new in the department, I cannot
impress on you enough the need for constantly
policing this list.

As you may or may not know, many of our top customers have more than one charge account. One may
be for wife and family, and six others may be for
friends and mistresses. It is imperative that each
and every Triple A charge card number be scrutinized
to see where the mail and bill should be sent. The
accounts are coded, and once you get the pattern
down it's relatively simple to hawk the list.

Last year one of our top customers charged a very
expensive fur coat. He used his code charge. Your
predecessor goofed and the charge went to the customer's home. I cannot tell you how unpleasant it
was, and we damn near had a lawsuit on our hands.

Give this immediate attention even if it means
overtime.

HN/bb

nevins markham

Fur letter from Mr. Harold Nevins to 2,300 Triple A list out of the city code

September 25, 1979

Dear Mr. _____,

I was so pleased to notice that despite the fact you haven't been in our fair city lately you are still using your charge account at Nevins Markham by employing our catalogues and mailing pieces. This delights me. As I looked over the many beautiful things coming up in our new catalogue, I wanted to suggest something very special for your wife's Christmas present.

As you probably have read, Ms. Hannah Nevins made a very astute move when she bought all the available Sablinka skins. Sablinka is a very special new fur, a cross between a Russian sable and a blue United States mink. This fur is the rarest and most expensive in the world.

I'm sending along a sketch of the coat and some of the shorter pieces that we will have on hand this Christmas. The coat is from Trigère--need I say more? If this interests you as a gift idea, let me know.

I hope you are in the best of health and that your business is prospering.

Sincerely,

Harold Nevins
President

HN/bb

nevins markham
elm and orchard
canyon city, texas 78254

Sept. 16, 1979

Mr. Stan King
Jacaranda Club
Canyon City, Texas

Dear Mr. King,

    This is to confirm per our phone conversation that Nevins Markham would like to reserve the Hibiscus Room for the entire evening of January 10, 1980. Cocktails will be served in the Magnolia Room, where our Display Department will set up easels, boards, sand, and spray. I promise you that the floor and carpets will be adequately covered by our display people, so there will be no unfortunate spills. Most of the people will be there by 6:30, and we want to give them until 8 P.M. to paint and drink. Then we can open the Hibiscus Room for dinner. I'm having Sue Ellen Anderson check the menu with M. Pierre. We'll have Indian-type music--snare drums and bongos or whatever they play--plus Bill Long for regular dancing. Ms. Anderson will give you a definite head count the Monday before on food. I'm sure we'll be talking more as we get closer to the date. Thanks for all your help.

                        Sincerely,

                        Penelope Smith
                        Advertising Manager

cc: Sue Ellen Anderson
    Isabella Montenegro
    TJ Bennis
    Jean Derujinski

PS/ps

Sept. 30, 1979

Dear Penelope,

Grandma called all excited about your birthday present and card. Why in God's name you would send Gran a reptile Kleenex holder beats me. You know she uses linen hankies. And she's against killing anything that's an endangered species. Both Aunt Amey and Gran are puzzled about your letters. I can't help much because it's obvious Darwin gets one set of news, Gran another, and me the third.

Believe it or not, we had a cold snap this weekend and Mr. Reynoldson came by and fertilized me in case of frost. Please let us know if you are coming home for Christmas. Aunt Amey is getting nudgy and wants to set the table and throw a sheet over it. Is it still on with you and Darwin and should Amey ask him? Love,

Mother

nevins markham

CONFERENCE REPORT   October 1, 1979

PRESENT   Harold Nevins, Isabella Montenegro, Tiny Halmark,
          Penelope Smith, TJ Bennis, Ethle Sideman, Carl
          Jurgen-Spitz, Hannah Nevins, Marina de Perigny, Sue
          Ellen Anderson, Jean Derujinski, Stella Branden, Bill
          Lance, Billy Sutton

SUBJECT   November Plans Board

          Ms. Montenegro reported on Sablinka and gave a review
          of all planned promotions. Carl Jurgen-Spitz
          cautioned all departments, especially Advertising
          and Display, on the advisability of being bonded for
          moving Sablinka skins. Sue Ellen Anderson, Jean
          Derujinski, and Tiny Halmark will also be bonded.
          Each person will report to Mr. Jurgen-Spitz for
          proper forms and fingerprinting.

          Ms. Montenegro showed her Carol Channing poster and
          received a round of applause.

          Ms. Montenegro reported on updated Mr. Mistletoe
          plans. Mr. Mistletoe will be promoted from November 5
          through November 12 with a series of teaser ads. The
          ads will be prepared by Ms. Smith with Ms. Branden.
          The Mistletoe cottage will be officially opened with
          Ms. Montenegro cutting the door out of the fern. Sue
          Ellen Anderson will arrange to have a reporter from
          each paper, and TJ Bennis will arrange for the fern
          to be cut. Ms. Montenegro suggested that TJ Bennis
          construct the Mistletoe house so that Frederico Lilac
          can get in it just before the press arrives. He will
          pop out just as Ms. Montenegro finishes cutting the
          door. Ms. Hannah wondered if this wasn't just a bit
          juvenile for a sophisticated store. But both Mr.
          Nevins and Ms. Montenegro felt it is just what NM
          needs to make the store a warmer, cheerier place at
          Christmas. Billy Sutton will work with Ms. Bennis in
          creating some way of using hidden camera equipment.
          Sue Ellen Anderson queried about remote-control TV
          for people and parents outside the cottage, but Ms.
          Montenegro felt this would take the mystique out of
          the average child's fantasy approach to the cottage
          of Mr. Mistletoe.

nevins markham

Mr. Nevins suggested that all promotional people think about his idea of creating a Nevins Markham cookbook. Ms. Montenegro thought the recipes should come from our own customers and is going to check out with Bob Sweeney the possibility of including an invitation to submit family recipes in the November mailing.

Ms. Montenegro suggested contacting Art Buchwald or Erma Bombeck for editing and writing the cookbook, but Ms. Anderson thought it should be more Canyon City-oriented and that the book would be overshadowed by big names.

Mr. Nevins will talk to Harcourt Brace Jovanovich re publishing it next year. Ms. Hannah thought the store should be able to move at least 10,000 cookbooks for Christmas 1980.

Ms. Anderson wanted to hold up on invitations for recipes until she could estimate the number of replies. Ms. Montenegro thought we should go ahead as quickly as possible and worry about the PR later. Mr. Nevins agreed.

Suggested titles should be submitted before the December Plans meeting to Ms. Montenegro.

Fur storage and remodeling plans were discussed and Ms. Hannah felt that more pressure should be used. An extra $10,000 was budgeted.

transcribed from tape by bb/

nevins markham
elm and orchard
canyon city, texas 78254

Oct. 8, 1979

Mr. Charles Chipmonk
The Cathedral Ranch
Santa Fe, New Mexico 87501

Dear Mr. Chipmonk,

Mr. Nevins told me that you are coming to
Canyon City on January 10. I'm delighted and I
will do all I can to make your stay a pleasant as
well as a profitable one. I've spent a lot of time
this week looking at your sand paintings owned by
Mr. Nevins. I must say the technique fascinates me,
and I hope someday to be able to afford my own
Chipmonk.

Sue Ellen Anderson, our Public Relations
Director, has asked that your PR people send her
any materials on you and photos. And I'd like to ask
you a big favor. Would you paint our first ad? I'll
run it the Sunday before your exhibition. I can use
four colors and the paper is quite good at matching
tones. If you design something, we could have a
poster made of it as a souvenir of your trip. Texans
are very sentimental, and it would be a great way
for them to start a collection of Chipmonks. And
once a Texan starts a collection he usually goes all
out.

We'll be sending you your complete itinerary
with press conferences, etc. I'll be in touch with
you again soon.

Sincerely yours,

Penelope Smith
Advertising Manager

PS/ps

nevins markham

October 9, 1979

Please give me a blow-by-blow description of
everything you have going to promote Sablinka. We
have an enormous investment in this coat and the
small pieces, and I haven't even had a bite.

HN/ub

nevins markham

Oct. 10, 1979

OK. I've had it! You have carried on long enough
over Display problems of security. What do you
suggest that's possible to follow through with? We
change all windows in all stores on Thursday night.
I cannot be in all stores on Thursday night. I am at
the downtown store on Thursday night. I have one kid
out at Swinburn and one kid at the International
Plaza. While they go in one window the rest of the
merchandise is open to any cleaning help or security
man (hmmmmm) to simply lift. If I can have extra
help to watch what's going into the station wagons
and coming back to downtown, I could feel a sense of
responsibility. But unless you and your force help,
this is impossible. Filling out your forms is not
only time-consuming--it's plain ridiculous when I
haven't a clue what <u>your</u> people have lifted.

cc: Harold Nevins
    Penelope Smith

Isabella Montenegro

Vice-President/Nevins Markham
Sales Promotion

October 11, 1979

To: Penelope Smith
    Bill Lance
    Sue Ellen Anderson
    TJ Bennis
    Jean Derujinski

Please give me a blow-by-blow description
of exactly what is being done in your
various departments to promote Sablinka.
I want this material on my desk on Monday
--in writing.

IM/rm

nevins markham

10/15/79

Dear Ms. Nevins,

It seems to me that the most important thing for
everyone's consideration re Sablinka is the bonding
of all the people who are not already bonded by our
own insurance company. As you know, with certain
policies bonding is automatic. But the bonding
people are difficult re bonding outside of regular
bonding. For ex: a model modeling the coat outside
the store not in a fashion show for which we are
explicitly bonded would have to be bonded. I believe
a meeting with all people who are going to handle
Sablinka in any way at all would be valuable. I will
set this meeting up at your convenience.

Oct. 17

Dearest Dar,

    A minor victory! I told you I got Chipmonk to
agree to paint his own ad. Monty will be out of town
for the Indian war dance so maybe I can do something
interesting and get my name on it. Anyway, last
night I ran into Harold Nevins leaving the store.
Jurgen-Spitz was chewing me out re a kid glove that
got lost. (I ate it!) When he sees Harold he turns
into a headwaiter at a Viennese chocolate shop.
"Gut eefning, Meester Nehhvins," he smarmies out.
So I got away easy. Harold asks if he can drop me. I
live on opposite side of town. But I tell him I'm
going to Villaloma. It's too good a chance to miss.
Well, we talk and I try to be honest. I tell him
about the creeps at the bank and how they ain't been
no father to me. And I tell him about Chipmonk's
free artwork. And he is very pleased. I get out in
Villaloma and hope to God there is a bus. There
isn't. So, 10 bucks for a taxi. But it was worth
every $$$ to get the old boy's ear.

    Well, this morning I'm writing up some
Ferragamos when in rips Isabeyyah. How dare I
order up promotional material without clearing it
with her? So I say, "Come again?" (I try to keep
all conversations with her to two-word questions.)
"Harold told me you had artwork from Chipmonk," she
growls. "Is that true?" I told her it was. So she
rips into me. Says she looked like a fool, had to
act like she knew all about it. And then she says

from the chipped chippendale desk of **Penny Smith**

silkily, "Oh, Smithey, what am I going to do with you?" And I couldn't resist, Dar. I said, "The important thing, Isabeyyah, is what are you going to do without me?" Well, that fried it. She literally spit it out. "Look, chickey-pie, your job is to come up with ideas. My job is to decide which ones are any good. And let me tell you, all your gems are not good." I could not resist. I told her that bad gems were better than no gems. Well, she slammed out, saying, "Don't push me too hard, Smithey. I can be <u>real</u> mean." I guess it was time to finally declare open warfare. I feel a lot happier.

I'm going to a football game this weekend. Sue Ellen has passes. She says Texas football is an experience. It will be if she hits the beer. Two swigs of Miller High Life and she'll be on the field. Oh, well, it's better than listening to Willie Pearl fiddle and Spot moan. Love,

Penny

from the chipped chippendale desk of Penny Smith

nevins markham

Oct. 16, 1979

Can you get any pictures from the tulip crowd that
show tulip beds? I have to order some huge container
beds to house them on ledges above the main floor,
and it would be helpful if I could see how they
arrange them. I know I could go to the library
but . . .

Canyon City Bank
(the bank that's like a father to you!)

October 19, 1979

Ms. Penelope Smith
Advertising Manager
Nevins Markham
Elm and Orchard
Canyon City, Texas 78254

Dear Ms. Smith:

Mr. Harold Nevins, a stockholder in the Canyon City Bank, and I had a discussion recently in which he questioned the bank's advertising policies. I must apologize. Your letter has indeed been sitting on my desk, but an answer to it has been uppermost in my mind. I am also sorry that you have had an unpleasant experience with our loan people. I've spoken with our Mr. Ross, and your car loan has been approved. Do please consider Canyon City Bank as a friend as well as a father to you. And please don't hesitate to get directly in touch with me any time you are unhappy with our service.

Please convey my best wishes to Mr. Harold Nevins.

Sincerely,

John H. Farrell, Jr.
President

JHF/on

nevins markham

advertising copy:

for cycle billing
November

WANTED! REWARD!

Nevins Markham is writing a Texas
cookbook and we want your recipes in it!
It can be Grandma's utterly deeelicious
pecan pie--with credit, of course, to
Grandma. It can be Uncle Sut's Red-Hot
Chili or Cowpoke's Stew. It can be your
own fabulous Key Lime Pie. Send us one or
send us ten recipes that are real Texas
cooking.

We hope to have big-time designers'
recipes, and we'll put them all in a
handsome cookbook in full color. So
hurry. Send your recipes in today. The
book will be published by Harcourt Brace
Jovanovich, Inc., next year. Mail all
entries to Public Relations Department,
Nevins Markham.

nevins markham
elm and orchard
canyon city, texas 78254

office of the president

October 26, 1979

Mr. William DelaCort
Queen's Ranch
Los Cocos, Texas

Dear Bill,

How are you, you ornery ole critter? I talked to
your new wife the other day when she was shopping
in the store. (You sure have great taste in women.)
She was telling me you are taking a cruise early in
the New Year. Well, Bill, I had a thought.

As you probably read in the Wall Street Journal, my
sister Hannah just grabbed up all the Sablinka skins
in the world. She practically took over the Rajah
Mink Farm (and she brought us the silkiest little
fellows you ever did see). Sablinka is a cross
between a sable and a mink, and it's a knockout.
It's damned expensive but worth every cent. We're
making up just one full-length coat. And it's a
dandy from a really fine New York designer. I'm
enclosing a sketch. This would be some present for
your wife. If you're interested, let me know as
we're sitting on some offers, but I'd a lot rather
you had it. There's going to be a lot of publicity
on the woman who ends up wearing Sablinka. I think
your wife would look great on TV.

Best wishes,

Harold Nevins

HN/bb

Sunday, November 4th

Dear Penny,

Just a line to say hello. We've had a big snow.
So much so that Mr. Reynoldson had to come shovel up
my front so I can get out to church. I'll mail
this on the way. I was so glad you sent Gran the
invitation to enter her chili recipe. I don't
believe a Mexican could beat that recipe. She's very
excited. You know how she responds to contests.
Well, no news here. I have my Christmas shopping all
done. Whatever happened to your mistletoe man? Amey
hasn't cut out a word on your store. You must be
slowing down. Love,

Mother

nevins markham

November 5, 1979

We've been having an enormous amount of first-class
mail delivered to the store since the first of the
month. Most of it is for the Public Relations
Department but Sue Ellen Anderson refuses to accept
it in her office. At first I thought some mistake
had occurred in the catalogue or the October mailing
cycle. But it is neither the catalogue nor the
mailing. It's the recipe insert we did in November,
and it is pulling better than any merchandise has in
years. To date we have approximately 80 bags. This
is not counting the six Ms. Anderson has in her
office. Ms. Anderson has requested that I ship all
this to Mrs. Montenegro, but I rather felt this
would not be protocol. Would you have some notion of
what to do with all this mail? I can sort out the
sacks, but we have no capacity here at the warehouse
for any mail that doesn't concern orders from the
catalogues. Please advise.

November 6, 1979

To: Harold Nevins

I don't want to be accused of being
negative (as I often am these days), but
after only five days of the November
cycle billing asking for Texas recipes my
office looks like the main post office at
Christmas. I have the world bank of
unopened letters. Please, I beg you--
cancel the rest of the cycle. Mrs.
Montenegro refuses to do this. I have
requested Bob Sweeney to send all the
mail to Mrs. Montenegro or at least to
keep it at the warehouse and start people
opening it out there. The cycle is up
to "H." No one wants to talk about
sorting this mail, answering this mail,
classifying this mail, and, finally,
tactfully rejecting 99% of this mail. I
believed your idea to do a regional
cookbook was a great idea. I still do.
But I do not think--and I have not
thought--that Mrs. Montenegro's whole-
hog approach to mailing lists was a good
idea. Thousands of our customers are not
going to understand why little ole Uncle
Sut's Polecat Pie was not good enough for
Nevins Markham. Please advise Mr. Sweeney
to hold everything.

cc: Mrs. Montenegro

Isabella Montenegro

Vice-President/Nevins Markham
Sales Promotion

November 7, 1979

To: Sue Ellen Anderson
    Penelope Smith

Once again I would like to remind you
that members of the promotion staff are
not to send memos on promotions to anyone
without clearing these memos with me.
This is my last warning.

IM/rm

Isabella Montenegro

Vice-President/Nevins Markham
Sales Promotion

November 7, 1979

To: Sue Ellen Anderson
    Penelope Smith

The easiest way to solve your problem (as
I see it) is to face the problem and do
the following in this order:

1. Open the mail.
2. Sort the recipes into regional and
   nonregional recipes. Get rid of all
   nonregional. Send a cute reject that
   will make people feel they were
   considered but didn't follow
   directions. Get Smithey to get one
   up fast.
3. Sort out what's left into various
   categories--i.e., soups, meats,
   vegetables, desserts, etc. Follow Joy
   of Cooking and you can't go wrong.
4. Smith can start writing copy about
   Tex-Mex food. I suggest that you both
   start reading some Texas history. Why
   not cover what Frank Tolbert and Dobie
   and McNeil have done on the Wild West?
   I have a darling story on hush
   puppies.
5. Get in touch with my good friend James
   Beard and see if he will test the
   recipes. If he doesn't want to do it,
   try my good friend Craig Claiborne.
6. Set a deadline for choosing the
   recipes. We have to be finished early
   in the spring. We must have the book
   ready for Christmas selling.

I know this demands a certain kind of
discipline. So let's get right at it.

cc: Harold Nevins

IM/rm

November 8, 1979

To: Isabella Montenegro

Your suggestions are just dandy. However,
I must emphasize once again that none
of this casual letter opening can take
place without some staff. I do not have
a staff. I have to cope with my day-to-
day duties and I'm loaded. I have Mr.
Mistletoe opening on the 23rd. I have
the press for Sablinka. I have Charlie
Chipmonk coming up. I have the Christmas
show. Penny has ads to do for every one of
these events plus the regular ads. There
isn't a snowball's chance of getting
anything sorted, opened, classified, or
written unless you can provide some
realistic help. As for James Beard or
Craig Claiborne, why don't <u>you</u> contact
your old friends?

cc: Harold Nevins

Isabella Montenegro

Vice-President/Nevins Markham
Sales Promotion

November 9, 1979

To: Sue Ellen Anderson
    Penelope Smith

I am appointing five students from Canyon
City University to work part-time until
the holidays and full-time during the
holidays. I will give them instructions
on how to sort and classify. Thus we can
end this amateur-night hysteria. As you
both know, we are riding a very tight
deadline as the publisher is rushing
the book through in order to have it
available for a major cookbook club which
is featuring regional cookbooks. So pull
yourselves together. This not only could
be a great public relations stunt, but it
should produce sales in our gourmet shop.

cc: H. Nevins

IM/rm

Marshall Field & Company

                                    Nov. 11, Veterans Day
Dear Penelope,

    Well, Darwin just called me and told me that
<u>you</u> are going to write the cookbook. That's
certainly an unusual thing for you to do since
you don't cook. Gran is terribly anxious that you
put her recipe in your book correctly. Now for
heaven's sake do that for her. She's not going to
live forever, you know.

    Of course, we're all disappointed that you're
not coming for Thanksgiving. Amey is having a
Butterball. What kind of store is that with no
holidays? Amey gets Thursday off and then she'll
take her regular Friday. That gives her a splendid
long weekend.

    I bought a new spread for your bed so your room
will look nice for you at Christmas. I must say it's
mighty quiet here with you gone. But we can't have
that argument again, can we? Have a nice holiday.
I'm counting on your calling home but try not to
call during dinner. They don't do much of anything
anymore for the poor veterans. I didn't even see a
poppy lady at church this morning. Love,

                                    Mother

nevins markham

November 13, 1979

It seems odd to me that although Nevins Markham
sells more fine furs than anyone else in the
Southwest, we have a singularly poor track record
on storing and remodeling furs. I think it's just
plain lack of promotion on the part of the store
and a lackluster attitude we all take here toward
service departments such as these.

Granted, they are not the high-glamour areas, but
they can be high-profit centers. And the profit is
in remodeling. Once you get a fur into the store for
storage, a customer can usually be tempted into
doing something with it. You've been so good at
coming up with creative ideas I wonder if you would
give this your full attention.

HN/ub

Isabella Montenegro

Vice-President/Nevins Markham
Sales Promotion

To: Sue Ellen Anderson

This just came from my good friend Chuck at <u>Life</u>. I want to get reprints for every employee in the store and all branches so they can take pride in my Mr. Mistletoe.

Famous Texas Store Gives the World A Whole New Fairy

<u>Life</u>, November 26, 1979

Nevins Markham must have coined the word "maverick," because they don't do anything the way other folks do. This year they dropped Santa Claus from their vocabulary in favor of a fairy. And Texas children have a chance to visit Mr. Mistletoe, a beautiful Puck-like fairy who lives in a fern and mistletoe house.

Mr. Mistletoe's house uses up 160 pounds of fresh mistletoe each week. When the kids arrive, Mr. Mistletoe gives them a giant fairy cookie (which brings good luck and ensures their getting the present of their dreams). And while little Bobby is talking away, a remote camera snaps his picture. Mommies and proud Daddies and adoring Grandmas can have a snap (for a fee, of course) of Mr. Mistletoe and the kids.

At week's end, over 4,000 children have been kissed by Mr. Mistletoe, who is none other than the famous Mr. Frederico Lilac of the Monaco Ballet. He's playing the role for an off-season lark.

Mr. Lilac says he just loves watching the children respond, and he reports that little boys seem to respond more to magic than little girls.

Mrs. Isabella Montenegro, author of the best-selling *Chic to Chic* and Vice-President of the famous Nevins Markham, says she got the idea for Mr. Mistletoe when Harold Nevins, President of Nevins Markham, said he wanted a new idea for a Christmas "myth."

December 3,1979

To the person in charge of

Mr.Mistletoe

Nevins Markham

Canyon City,Texas 78254

To whom it may concern:

    As a special treat I took my children
and my neighbor's children (nine in all) to
see your Mistletoe Fairy. Three of our little
boys had the same problem with your Fairy. I
don't believe you ought to employ such a
person.

    You should do something about this
right away. I am shocked.

        Yours very truly,

        Mrs.Hardeneda Ramsdell

nevins markham

elm and orchard
canyon city, texas 78254

Dec. 4, 1979

Mrs. Hardeneda Ramsdell
1078 N. Lomo Vista
Canyon City, Texas 78254

Dear Mrs. Ramsdell,

Your letter came to my attention today, and
you may rest assured that we will act immediately.
I'm most grateful that you alerted us. We are sorry
beyond belief that your little boy had a negative
reaction to Mr. Mistletoe. Perhaps we can make it up
to him. Next time you are in the store, please call
me and I will see that he gets a pretty new toy to
remember Nevins Markham by.

Sincerely yours,

Penelope Smith
Advertising Manager

cc:Sue Ellen Anderson

PS/ps

Dec. 4

to: Sue Ellen Anderson

Listen. Monty's gone off to collect her
just awards for the best advertising of
the year and we are beginning to get
screwie mail. Re: Mister Mistletoe. I
answered the first one, figuring she
was a nut, but now I have letter 2. What
do I do? If I report to the old boy,
Isabeyyah will say I should have called
her. Besides, if we're wrong, we could be
sued from here to heaven by Mr. Mistletoe. Can I shift this mail onto you and
stay out of it?

from the chipped chippendale desk of Penny Smith

Dec. 4

to: Billy Sutton

You've been snapping the kids in Mr.
Mistletoe's cottage. Have you noticed
anything weird going on? I got a letter
today that has me worried. Call me as
soon as you get in.

from the chipped chippendale desk of Penny Smith

December 4, 1979

Nevins Markham
Elm and Orchard
Canyon City, Texas 78254

To whom it may concern:

My husband is going to come down and
punch you and your fairy right in the
face. This will be for what he did to my
six-year-old son, Roy. Disgraceful. You
should all be ashamed of yourselves. I
suppose you think it's chic. Well, it's
not.

Sincerely,

Mrs. Horatio de Bartonio

ANITA RICHTER

Dec. 5, 1979

Nevins Markham
Elm & Orchard
Canyon City, Tex. 78254

Dear Sirs,

I really don't know how to write this letter, but I feel that it is my duty. I am a schoolteacher in Marble Falls, and as a special reward to my students for their good behavior I brought the entire fourth grade to see your much-publicized Mistletoe Fairy. Well!

On the way home in the bus I heard the children talking and I isolated a few. I could not believe my ears. That fairy should not be in touch with children--fourth grade or younger, fourth grade or older. Now I know that children tend to be excitable and often exaggerate, but in this case I believe they are telling the truth.

I would just as soon not call attention to this publicly for the children's sake only. If you will do something about this right away, I'll keep my peace. But should you fail to change this situation, I will have to take steps so that other teachers, parents, and children will not undergo this experience.

Please advise me as soon as you take action. My phone number is 311-555-3572.

Sincerely,

Anita Richter
107 Nightingale Rd.
Marble Falls, Tex.

From the desk of

Sue Ellen Anderson
Public Relations/Nevins Markham

December 5, 1979

To: Mr. Nevins

Mrs. Montenegro is out of town and some
letters came to my attention re Mr.
Mistletoe that I found very disturbing. I
don't know Mr. Lilac personally and I
think you should see these letters.
Please advise.

From the desk of

Sue Ellen Anderson
Public Relations/Nevins Markham

December 5

To: Penny Smith

God! Let's get right to Mr. N. Forget
your Isabeyyah hangup. This is serious.
I've made a date for 11. Lance says
you're out roaming the store. Call me
immediately.

Diamonds? Never!

Sablinka is a girl's best friend!

Is it possible Carol Channing has changed her sparkling mind? You bet! Status symbols change and this year Sablinka (that beautiful cross between Russian sable and U.S. mink) has moved into the #1 spot. Sablinka is better than a kiss on the hand (or even one on the lips), and because it was designed by the famous Trigère it is definitely Continental. See how very chic it looks on Ms. Channing. Now shut your eyes and just visualize how it will look on you. Then if there is some gentleman out there who is eager to please you this Christmas, just tell him what a girl's best friend really is. Sablinka. The one and only one in the whole wide world. 100,000.00

nevins markham

Golden Key to Nevins Markham

NEW YORK—Nevins Markham of Canyon City, Texas, captured the highly prized Golden Key for the best retail advertising of the year. They also walked off with a special blue ribbon for their Sablinka promotion which featured a one-of-a-kind coat.

"The Sablinka promo was a shoo-in," said Isabella Montenegro, Vice-President and Sales Promotion Director of the store. "Once we had the famous Carol Channing smile behind us, how could we miss?"

When Ms. Montenegro ac-cepted the award on behalf of Nevins Markham at the Golden Key dinner held at the Hilton, she tucked the key in her bosom and sang, "For us female retailers gold keys are a girl's best friend."

nevins markham

December 6, 1979

Without upsetting the publicity we've had on Mr.
Mistletoe, I want you to discreetly terminate
Mr. Frederico Lilac's contract with us through
Christmas Eve. This is a very touchy situation.
Just take it on my word that we want to substitute
one of our own people for the Mistletoe Fairy. Sue
Ellen Anderson has found Mrs. Louise Adelberry, an
alterations assistant who has recently retired from
our staff. She's delighted to put the costume on and
be with the children until Christmas. I'm sure you
will find a tactful and careful way to terminate Mr.
Lilac. I'd like him off the premises immediately.

cc: Isabella Montenegro, NY office
    Sue Ellen Anderson

HN/bb

nevins markham

December 7, 1979

Dear Penelope,

Mr. Nevins has always believed in rewarding those people in the store who have done an especially good job by sending them a special Christmas bonus. I'm enclosing your check.

Since we know that many of our employees like to clear up their charge account balances for the year and start the new year fresh, our Payroll Department has deducted your balance.

Merry Christmas and a Happy New Year!

NAME	EMP. NO.	PERIOD ENDING	TIME WORKED	RATE	Bonus	REGULAR	O.T.	OTHER	TOTAL	W. TAX	F.I.C.A.	S.W.T.	CHG. ACCT.	TOTAL	NET PAY
Penelope Smith	72	12/31						1000.00	1000.00	375.85	61.30	25.00	536.38	1000.00	1.47

EARNINGS	★	DEDUCTIONS

DETACH THIS STUB BEFORE CASHING.

nevins markham
elm and orchard
canyon city, texas 78254

No 12456

0-00
000

DATE December 7, 1979

PAY TO THE
ORDER OF   Penelope Smith

00,00¢ 1¢¢47¢¢¢ $1.47

_____ DOLLARS

Canyon City Bank
Canyon Plaza, Canyon City, Texas 78254

Woodward Frowles

⑆0000⑈0000⑇ 12345⑈678⑈9 0⑈

nevins markham

December 8, 1979

I'm sending along several clippings from various
stores on how they have handled contests, etc., on
fur storage and remodeling. Let me know what you
think.

HN/ub

nevins markham

inter-office memo

to: Ms. Hannah Nevins

from: Harry Sutter, Furs

Dec. 13, 1979

I just wanted to let you know and make you aware of
the fact that we haven't even had a nibble on the
Sablinka pieces. We've got such an investment here
it's hurting. I've got a hot short lynx jacket I'd
like to place an order on, but I have no open to buy
because of all the Sablinka. If we don't sell the
full-length coat, have you thought about how we will
handle it as a mark-down? Since we had all this
publicity, I kind of hate to mark it down publicly.
Please advise.

Dec. 17, 1979

to: Isabella Montenegro

Mr. Sutter wants to know if you have
some ideas on how to place the Sablinka
pieces in the after-Christmas sale. He's
worried. He doesn't know whether to play
it up or play it down. Do you want up
or down? Maybe now is the time for
"sensational."

from the chipped chippendale desk of Penny Smith

From the desk of

Sue Ellen Anderson
Public Relations/Nevins Markham

December 20, 1979

To: Harold Nevins

I hear that Bill DelaCort is thinking
very seriously about the Sablinka. I have
a far-out idea that's expensive, but it
might work. Why don't I call Howie
Silvers, get him to ship a beautiful Sablinka pelt to us air, and I'll get Penny
Smith to design a Christmas greeting card
built all around Lil DelaCort. We'll ship
the card and gift box to Bill DelaCort,
and chances are he'll have five bourbons
on Christmas Eve, get maudlin, and give
Mrs. D. the card. Once we get that far,
the coat should be right behind.

cc: Penny Smith

nevins markham

December 27, 1979

DelaCort bought Sue Ellen's pelt. Sablinka has been sold. I had to give him the projected 20% off but at least we can save face and not have to put the coat on sale. And we got a lot of mileage out of that purchase. I promised Bill that we'd get publicity on Mrs. DelaCort wearing the Sablinka. Now we can think of some way to move the smaller pieces. I'm dead set against putting them on sale publicly. I think it destroys our fashion and taste credibility.

HN/bb

nevins markham
elm and orchard
canyon city, texas 78254

21478-32

686	SEND TO	

SEND TO
MRS. W. Dela Cort

STREET
Queen's Ranch

CITY Los Cocos, **STATE** Texas

AREA	SALES NO.	DATE	KIND OF SALE	IF C.O.D. COLLECT
37	HOUSE	12/27/9	CHG.	

PURCHASED BY
X V. Dela Cort

CHARGE TO
N-M ACCOUNT NO. 252-013-532-4

MR. W. Dela Cort
STREET Queen's Ranch
CITY Los Cocos, Texas

DEPT.	CLASS	QUAN.	ARTICLE	PRICE	AMOUNT	
37		1	Floor Length Sablinka	Adj.	80,000	00
			alter sleeves deliver to ranch no later than 1/10		—	—
					—	—

AUTH. SIGNATURE SFC **TOTAL** ▶ 80,000 00

DELIVERY CHARGES INCLUDE POSTAGE, PACKING, HANDLING AND INSURANCE.

AUDITOR'S VOUCHER

AREA	SALES NO.	DATE	KIND OF SALE	AMT. REC'D	AMT. SALE

nevins markham
elm and orchard
canyon city, texas 78254

21478-32

From the desk of

Sue Ellen Anderson
Public Relations/Nevins Markham

                                    December 28, 1979

        To: Harold Nevins
            Isabella Montenegro

        Speaking of fashion credibility, do you
        really want Ms. Hannah's Sablinka draped
        across the siliconed bosoms of Bill
        DelaCort's latest?

(No, I don't have a new
job at Field's. I'm
just using Mama's stash
of stationery.)

Dec. 28

Dear Sue Ellen,

    I love my "Isabeyyah" dart board! I hung it
across from my bed, and while I have my coffee each
morning I plan to throw darts at the most painful
places. Thank you for this marvelous release.

    Home is home. What can I say? Aunt Amey had
seven strays from all walks of life for Christmas
dinner, and Mama was furious because they all
glommed onto the dark meat which is all Mama likes.
I told them all the story about the woman who got
her Christmas present with the gift wrapper's
sandwich in it.

    Aunt Amey's friend Mae Carnes (who sells
hosiery at Field's) told us about a spill she had
off the LeHigh bus. Seems she was standing on the
treadle, and when the bus stopped Mae fell out and
went sailing into a snowbank. The bus drove off. And
as Aunt Amey says, "If it hadn't been for Mae's
black galoshes, we might not have found her 'til
spring."

    I'm having a wonderful time with Darwin. He is
as adorable as he was in June and in a way I'm
closer to him now. I am doing my best to coax him
into trying his career in another state--like
Texas--but you know that means new bars, etc.
Anyway, I'm going to make a New Year's resolution
that "Montenegro will not bother me in the 80s." I
ought to be able to make it 'til the 2nd of Jan.
Have a happy one, old dear. I couldn't have made the
scene at all without you. Love,

        Penny

p.s. Gran gave me 10 Susan B. Anthony dollars with
    a note: "Buy anything your heart desires."
    Shouldn't she be on the "Triple A" list? Aunt
    Amey says if people didn't have faces she
    simply could not tell them apart!

Isabella Montenegro

Vice-President/Nevins Markham
Sales Promotion

December 31, 1979

To: Harold Nevins

Dear Hal,

Even though we're short-handed here
(Smithey is off playing), I just want to
go on record that I believe we <u>can</u> get
publicity on Lil DelaCort and the
Sablinka. After all, we bought Sablinka
for that very reason. It's always a
breeze to get good coverage on Cheryl
Tiegs types--it's hard work to pull it
off on a Lil. However, I can dredge up an
old contact who does publicity for the
<u>Queen Elizabeth II</u>. The DelaCorts are
taking a suite. They're going as far as
the Pacific and then they are flying
back. I think we can round up a story on
the luxury tie-in. Everyone loves to read
about money. I'll try Liz Smith and Suzy,
and if we take decent photos of the suite
we ought to be able to swing <u>Town &
Country</u>, the <u>News</u>, etc.

cc: Sue Ellen Anderson
    Hannah Nevins

IM/rm

```
For          Mrs. Montenegro

Date         12/31        Time   2  P.M.

WHILE YOU WERE OUT
M              Harold  Nevins

From

Phone No.
          Area Code        Number        Extension

| TELEPHONED | x | URGENT | |
| PLEASE CALL | | WANTS TO SEE YOU | |
| WILL CALL AGAIN | | CAME TO SEE YOU | |
| RETURNED YOUR CALL | | | |

Message   He says great.  Head for
          New York as soon as you
          can and meet the
          DelaCorts.


                          Rosemae
                            Operator
```

JA 3

Jan. 2, 1980

Dearest,

Well, I made it back. The airport was crazy. I hated to leave you. I love my bracelet. It's a beauty. We are a beautiful couple. And did you notice Mama's mouth drop open when you mentioned we are going to Haiti "together"? I am beginning to make plans right now for my Tulip Caper. I sat down with a calendar (and all the tulip correspondence) and I think I can cut the second the first batch of tulips arrives. There's an eight o'clock flight to Miami. Before I leave, I'm going to take all the tulip files home and let Isabeyyah sail around saying, "Not to worry, ya, ya." She stole this idea so long ago that she's really forgotten about it. I keep feeding her little bits of info that make her feel that she's on top of everything. Well, sweet, I also have to get cracking on Charlie Chipmonk.

I just loved seeing you, and I am having withdrawal symptoms something awful. Take care. I love you wildly.

Penny

from the chipped chippendale desk of Penny Smith

western union   # Telegram

78210 GS YT CANYONCITY TX 1-28 10:30A CST
MR AND MRS WILLIAM CLOHESY
1023 SOUTH MARIETTA ST
CANYONCITY TX 78232
YOU ARE CORDIALLY INVITED TO
AN EXHIBITION OF MR CHARLES CHIPMONK S NEWEST
COLLECTION OF UTE SAND PAINTINGS AND TO JOIN
MS HANNAH NEVINS FOR COCKTAILS AND DINNER AT
THE JACARANDA CLUB ON THURSDAY JANUARY 10, 1980
AT 7PM RSVP 555-0500, EXT 150. SUE ELLEN ANDERSON
OYBKUC RELATIONS DIRECTOR NEVINS MARKHAM

SF-1201 (R5-69)

Jan. 3

to: TJ Bennis

I just talked to Stan King and everything
is set. Your kids will have the Hibiscus
Room from right after lunch until 6 P.M.
to set up work tables and painting
equipment and the sand. I think letting
the guests have a hand at the art is a
great idea. King wants the floors and
rugs carefully covered, and, of course,
Jurken-Spitz wants the tables and brushes
counted before the party and after. I
think we should count the guests that
way. Sue Ellen thinks the women are more
likely to take a crack at painting than
the men. Her suggestion is to keep most
of the easels set at 5'5" and a few of
them at 5'10". We also want to hang some
of Charlie's work around the room, and
you'd better check you-know-who re
bonding. Also, Mr. Nevins wants to show
three of his own paintings. They are at
his house. Do you send Carl's Dobermans
out for them or what? As you know, the
telegram is just out, so we won't have
the numbers down for a couple of days.
Any other problems--just holler.

cc: Sue Ellen Anderson
    Jean Derujinski

from the chipped chippendale desk of Penny Smith

nevins markham

to: Sue Ellen Anderson, Penelope Smith

from: Harold Nevins

January 4, 1980

As soon as you get Chipmonk out of the way, I want
you both to get started on the cookbook. Do we have
a title? This is a priority.

HN/bb

First Sunday of the New Year

Dear Penelope,

Well, it was certainly nice having you home at last. Only God knows I didn't see much of you. I suppose it's normal for you to want to spend time with your contemporaries. Just what am I supposed to think of you and Darwin? Am I supposed to look the other way when you decide to stay out all night? And then I hear you are vacationing with Darwin. Now he is a nice young man. But you two are not married, and I don't think you should take trips together. When I went on vacation--before I married your father--I went with Jessie Minech or Susan Sullivan. They were just as nice to travel with as anyone I ever met. So give your life some deep thought. Is this what you really want to do? You know, men can just walk away unscathed. But women do not walk away. Well, enough of that. I got it off my chest and hopefully onto yours.

If you don't mind too much, I'm going to send the lovely electric blanket back to you for credit. I can't help myself, but I feel that anyone who can't manufacture their own heat in bed doesn't deserve to live. I'd like to have one of those Answer Blankets they advertise so much. In pale blue. Aunt Amey loves her earrings and Gran has worn nothing but your sweater since Christmas. Love,

Mother

From the desk of

Sue Ellen Anderson
Public Relations/Nevins Markham

                                    January 7, 1980

       To: Penny Smith

       We are sure not getting any results on
       Chipmonk's show. It's hard to bomb the
       people out of their plantations in
       January. A lot of top customers are
       in Florida or Mexico. Maybe we should
       broaden the list. I think it will have to
       be a phone bank. Do you think we should
       take the gnomes off the recipes, give
       them a prepared speech, and have them
       start calling? What even is a
       "priority"? Advise.

nevins markham
elm and orchard
canyon city, texas 78254

For immediate release: January 9, 1980

Contact: Sue Ellen Anderson, Nevins Markham

Charles Chipmonk flew into Canyon City today to officially open an exhibition of his famous sand paintings at Nevins Markham. It is the first public showing of Chipmonk's paintings in this country.

Charles Chipmonk lived on a reservation where art supplies did not exist. When he was eight, he began painting with sand and was discovered by John Healy, the famous architect, who enrolled him in the Institute of Art in Santa Fe. At 37, Chipmonk, Chief of the Thundering Pony Tribe, holds an M.A. in anthropology from the University of New Mexico. He regularly exhibits his work at the Utterman Gallery in London.

The collection at Nevins Markham marks his first use of mud with sand. On Thursday, January 10, at 1 P.M., Chipmonk will work on a large canvas in the NM gift shop. He plans to finish the painting on Friday. Students from ten art schools in the Southwest will observe Chipmonk at work. Nevins Markham will donate the finished canvas to Canyon City's Modern Museum.

The Chipmonk paintings will be shown at the Nevins Markham Gift Gallery through February.

Oh, Dar! My Chipmonk party was a first-class fiasco! Charlie arrived in his own plane and couldn't have been nicer. Sue Ellen and I took him to lunch and then got him set up in the Gift Gallery. But from two to four o'clock <u>not one soul</u> showed up. Oh, that's wrong. One lady asked him where the bathroom was. Sue Ellen phoned to see what had happened to the art students and discovered they had the wrong date. So she decided to get Chipmonk back to his hotel for a break before the party.

When I got to the Jacaranda Club, my heart sank. I don't know what list Bob Sweeney used, but the place looked like therapy class at the nursing home. There was not a soul under 70. Ms. Hannah kept tapping her foot. All of a sudden Sue Ellen and Charlie came staggering in--and I mean staggering. Charlie was on cloud nine and Sue was in outer space. I rushed her to the ladies' room and bribed the maid to lock her in. When I got back, Charlie had Bob Long playing some kind of mad music. Drunk or not, Charlie was having a great party. And the sweet old guests decided they loved tossing handfuls of sand into the air. Then they actually revived the Conga line. Charlie danced. Charlie talked. Charlie charmed. Charlie painted. As a finale he lifted Ms. Hannah right off her chair and swung her around the room. I don't think she has moved this fast in years. If Charlie hadn't slipped on a Caesar salad while jumping over a table (which he almost cleared), I think he'd be jiving it up still.

He never showed today. But all the students did. The Jacaranda Club is suing the store for

from the chipped chippendale desk of Penny Smith

sand damage. Chipmonk is suing the club for
Caesar salad damage, and I suppose Hannah Nevins
will sue me for ruining the store's image. I
need a smart lawyer.

Desolate Penny

P.S. Clip from today's paper. Give it to Aunt
Amey so she won't clip me one and send it to
me.

LIZ BROWN
Canyon Chatter

A lot of sand was kicked up at the posh Jacaranda Club last night when super-chic Hannah Nevins threw a bash for Charles Chipmonk, sand painting chief from Santa Fe. Stan King, Jacaranda's major domo, said he'd thrown a lot of parties in his day but nothing like Chipmonk's. "It will take years to find all the sand." Guests included the Bradford Armstrongs, Gillian Wentworth and her current one, Ellison and Babes Baxt, and Howard and Buffy Lovinson.

from the chipped chippendale desk of Penny Smith

nevins markham

January 14, 1980

In the future we will serve only wine at all store
functions. The bar is to be closed immediately after
dinner. If it's a cocktail party only, the bar will
be open for one hour and a half. I expect employees
not to imbibe at official store functions.

cc: Hannah Nevins

HN/bb

nevins markham

to: Isabella Montenegro

from: Hannah Nevins

January 14, 1980

I do hope you haven't put aside plans to do a major
push on fur storage.

HN/ub

Isabella Montenegro

Vice-President/Nevins Markham
Sales Promotion

January 15, 1980

Smithey. I thought you were going to take
over the fur storage package. Ms. Hannah
has seen no plans. Please take care of
this immediately. This is a priority.

IM/rm

Isabella Montenegro

Vice-President/Nevins Markham
Sales Promotion

January 21, 1980

To: Sue Ellen Anderson
    Penelope Smith

Please arrange your schedules so that you can both leave on January 26. I've made arrangements for you at the Bandito Ranch in Bandito, Texas, for one week. I believe this is sufficient time to put the cookbook to bed. I've also arranged for the Food and Nutrition Department of Canyon City University to test our recipes. See, Sue Ellen, nothing is impossible!

IM/rm

nevins markham

inter-office memo

to: Mr. Harold Nevins, Mrs. Isabella Montenegro

from: Carl Jurgen-Spitz, Security

1/23/80

I've made a list of all the merchandise signed
out to Advertising, Display, and Fashion for the
Christmas period that is still out. Could I have
some advice on how to handle this? It amounts to
several thousand dollars.

Isabella Montenegro

Vice-President/Nevins Markham
Sales Promotion

January 24, 1980

Dear Hal,

Since I'll be in Houston for a couple of days (doing my little bit for the Women in Communications group), I wanted to update you on all our little problems.

Sue Ellen is in the doghouse and she knows it! If you're as mad as I am she can stay there for a while. That Chipmonk affair was a disgrace. Now--my feelings re the cookbook. I wash my hands of the whole deal and I'm sure you will understand. I have thought all along that Erma or Art should write it. As it looks now, Sue Ellen is angling to get her name on the book jacket. Naturally, her pal Smith will go along with her on anything. But then I suppose this is a customer service kind of book and regional is regional. I wouldn't be surprised if the publisher just turns it down flat. Well, at least they're going to Bandito. Mrs. Klein, the owner, is a dear friend of mine and is a total teetotaler. So at least you won't have "that" worry on your hands. Otherwise, all goes well. My very best,

Isabella

IM/rm

Isabella Montenegro

Vice-President/Nevins Markham
Sales Promotion

January 25, 1980

Dear Hal,

Here are my first clips on the Sablinka sailing. I think,
all things considered, they're pretty good.

Mrs. Bill DelaCort of the famous Queen's Ranch
photographed in the beautiful one-of-a-kind Sablinka
coat. She and Bill DelaCort are cruising on the *Queen
Elizabeth II*. Nothing but the best for the Queen's Ranch
hands.

nevins markham

inter-office memo

to: Sydney Zucker, Isabella Montenegro

from: Hannah Nevins

January 25, 1980

Please don't forget to mention that we do fine fur
remodeling as well as storage in any advertising you
do. In fact, we should emphasize this in some way.

HN/ub

Dear Mama,
    The ranch is very nice.
The food is good, although
when you write about it
all day you sure don't
wan't to eat it at night.
    I've got Gran's recipe in and
I've spelled her name
    correctly. ent riding
and can hardly move.
        LOVE, Penny

POST CARD
Address

Mrs. D. Smith
8518 W. Winston Drive
Chicago, ILL.
    60611

Dear T J,
No Spitz!
No Sand!

Sue Ellen gets a little
restless at the cocktail
hour, but I think we'll
make it. LOVE from the
Queen of the Thundering
        Pony Tribe

POST CARD
Address

TJ Bennis
Nevins Markham
Elm t Orchard
Canyon City
TEXAS · 78254

Dear Dar,

Writing part-time and trying to keep Sue Ellen off the peyote full-time. This place is so far out it's called Gulag Bandito. Monty's no fool. Home next Mon. I hope. LOVE and wish you were really here.

Penny

Mr. Darwin Pace
Griffin, Greenwald,
Garamello + Sharpless
55 E. Monroe
Chicago, ILL.
60603

Dear Aunt Amey,

You ought to be in charge here.

EVERY dish has a chip in it and EVERY glass is cracked — but then it is a working ranch. Tell Gran her chili is right up front. Love,
P.

Ms. Amey Hennessey
Fine China + Glassware Dep't
COMPLAINTS
Marshall Field + Co.
Chicago, ILL.
60611

Tuesday

Penny/dearest nut Thanks fopr the
picturepostal from Bandits Ranch. By
theway . . . did you evetr get some kindof
xxx agreement that you and Sue would
share in the cook book royalties? Let me
know everything. Lov   Dar

nevins markham

inter-office memo

to: Penny Smith, Sue Ellen Anderson, Jean Derujinski

from: TJ Bennis

February 7, 1980

I have a "disposal" plan for Carl Jurgen-Spitz. I need your complete cooperation.

Penny—you get Spitz to lunch. Make him explain forms to you. Keep him out of his office for no less than 55 minutes. If he leaves for any reason, contact Sue Ellen.

Sue Ellen—you watch the hall. If Spitz appears for any reason, detain him. Send Rosemae to his office instantly. We'll clear out.

Jean—have several mannequins ready to be dressed. Place them near Spitz's office. Tag them Display. I will load them on top of all his furniture. Bring canvas from runway.

As I see it, Spitz hasn't varied his lunch hour in the past two weeks. We've clocked him. He arrives at the employees' cafeteria at 1:15 and he stays 'til 1:40. If they have chocolate pie he takes another five minutes. We need this time. I have the key to Spitz's office. My two assistants will wear painter's clothes and remove all his furniture, detach light fixture and phone, roll up carpet and place in hall. I will load it up in a dolly, place mannequins on top, cover with canvas, and have trucked to dead storage. It will be the first time in history a store dick has his office stolen. Let's try it Monday.

CARL JURGEN-SPITZ
LEAVES SECURITY POST
AT NEVINS MARKHAM

CANYON CITY, Feb. 15 — Carl Jurgen-Spitz announced his resignation today as Security chief at Nevins Markham.

Since Spitz joined Nevins Markham he has instituted many new security systems in the store. He hopes to announce his future plans within the week.

Spitz was formerly security officer at Gamble's department store in Pittsburgh, Pa.

Feb. 22

to: TJ Bennis

I just got word from the bulb guys that
the tulips will arrive on Invoice #735
from New York via Dutch Air on March 20
at 4 P.M. They'll come into the regular
air freight hangar. There should be
approximately 50 crates. The growers
suggest that you get your people to
cut the stems as the attached drawing
indicates. They are also sending potting
stuff that keeps the flowers happier. The
bulb man has your name as contact. They
suggest that you use a couple of inches
of lukewarm water when you first plunge
the darlings' feet into containers. It
seems they do not like cold feet. Maybe
that's my problem. I've been plunged too
often.

from the chipped chippendale desk of Penny Smith

DUTCH
BULB
GROWERS
(nothing like a Holland Tulip)

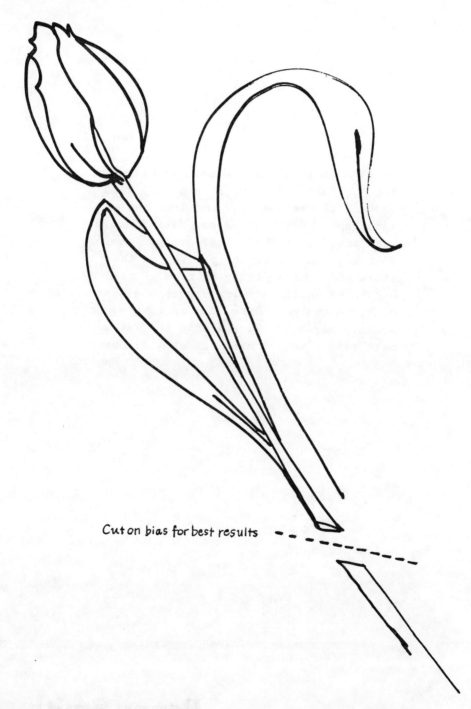

Cut on bias for best results

herengracht 392—amsterdam—telefoon 434355

Feb. 23

Dear Mama,

　　The cookbook is finished and gone to the publisher. I think it's a very good book. I'll see that you and Gran get an autographed copy. The store dick I hated has left. Isn't that nice? Are you coming down soon? I'd love for you to see the store and I have plenty of room. I will be back from Haiti (I'm leaving on the 21st of March and yes, Darwin is going too) on Sunday, March 30. Pick a date and let's make some plans. I miss you et all. Love,

　　　　　　　　　　　　　　Penny

from the chipped chippendale desk of Penny Smith

CERTIFIED COLD STORAGE

Name____DelaCort____

Description____Gray-Blue Mink____

Value____$80,000____

nevins markham
elm and orchard
canyon city, texas 78254

↓ *Indicate cleaning by placing **C** here*

FURRIER'S NO.____706____ | VAULT NO. | C | 201

FURRIER'S NO.____706____ | VAULT NO. | C | 201

Name____Mrs. W. DelaCort____

Description____Full-Length Coat____

Value____$80,000____

nevins markham

inter-office memo

to: Penelope Smith

from: TJ Bennis

Feb. 28, 1980

I know you're pulling out of here in a
couple of weeks. Can you clue me and Sue
Ellen into who gets what credits on the
tulips? The airlines. The government. The
artists. The poster. Maybe we'd better
have a quick meeting.

nevins markham
elm and orchard
canyon city, texas 78254

March 4, 1980

Mrs. W. DelaCort
Queen's Ranch
Los Cocos, Texas

Dear Mrs. DelaCort,

Your gray-blue mink coat was brought to my
personal attention the other day when it arrived to
be put in the fur storage vault. I'd like to tell
you what I think can be done to make this coat into
an exciting new fashion.

The fur is beginning to show wear at the hem
and at all the buttonholes. I'd like to suggest that
we shorten the coat for you to just below the knees
and repair the buttonholes. I believe we could give
you back enough mink for you to make two very nice
pillows. If you agree, I'll be happy to send out a
couple of drawings for you to see how your coat can
look for next fall.

We have one of the finest fur-remodeling
studios in the Southwest. Anytime you would like to
see it, please do not hesitate to call me. Awaiting
your approval, I remain,

Sincerely,

Sydney Zucker
Vice-President
Fur Storage and Remodeling

SZ/jl

March 13

to: Sue Ellen

OK. Here's the credit list:

TULIPS   Dutch Bulb Growers

                        Slogan—if you can tuck it in—
                        "Nothing like a Holland Tulip"

                        I've covered this a lot in the
                        ads so it's not imperative, but
                        if you can slip it into the main
                        release Ya Ya Klahorn will die a
                        happy man.

CLOTHES RESOURCES   Jean Derujinski has list

AIRLINES   Dutch Air

GOVERNMENT   We can throw a bouquet to Juliana
                        if you like or to all of Holland
                        for discovering the windmill.

                        Ya. Ya.   Penny

cc: Isabella Montenegro

March 14

to: Isabella Montenegro

The tulips are all arranged for. We'll
receive 75,000 to start. There's a hold
on 50,000 more, which will be force-
bloomed when TJ needs them. TJ has all
shipping instructions for clipping,
temperature, etc. All varieties will
be marked so Display can match their
interior signs with the labels on the
tulips.

The ads are all in the finish stage if you
want to take a look tomorrow. I think
they look great. Branden outdid herself.
All things being equal, I think you will
have a grand promotion even though I will
not be with you. You do remember I'm
leaving for Haiti right after the tulips
are installed. Your own little Dutch Girl
Penelope Smith will be back on tulip turf
March 31.

Ya Ya

from the chipped chippendale desk of Penny Smith

March 17

to: TJ Bennis

As you know, I'm leaving Friday for
Haiti. I can't think of a tulip left
uncut. For your records--if there is
anything you want to know, ask now.
Rosemae has the tulip file. Ya. Ya.
Bye. Bye.

     Penny

P.S. I'll be here 'til 6 P.M. Friday.

cc: Isabella Montenegro

from the chipped chippendale desk of **Penny Smith**

March 20

Dear Aunt Amey,

　　Gosh, it's been all too long since I wrote to
you and Gran. But here's a marvelous story to make
it up to you!

　　Remember the "Sablinka" coat I did the big
promotion on with Carol Channing? Well, we finally
sold it for a cool 80 G's to a wealthy Texas rancher
who had just married his sixth blonde. (He owns a
ranch 1/2 the size of Texas.) Anyway, it wasn't
easy. Lots of publicity. Everyone fought over the
Carol Channing posters but no one fought over the
Sablinka. So Lil DelaCort goes off on a big cruise
wearing the new Sablinka and gets her picture taken
for all the magazines. So far so good.

　　Now meanwhile, back at the store, they have
hired a new guy to beef up the Fur Remodeling
Department. (This plus furs is Ms. Hannah Nevins's
baby.) Well, she gives orders for him to write to
every single customer who stores a coat with us and
tell them that their coat looks old hat and worn.
Mr. Zucker does his job well. He writes to Lil and
tells her her coat is really out of date but he can
fix it fast and make her look chic as all get-out.

　　The proverbial hit the fan. Mrs. DelaCort
drives right into town, gets her coat out of
storage, walks in on Mr. Nevins <u>un</u>announced, and
dumps the Sablinka on the floor. And so we have that
wonderful one-of-a-kind coat back in our lives.

　　Aunt Amey, if you let me know right away, I
think I could get it for you at 1/2 price (50 G's).
I'm alerting you first. Well, that's my news. Mama
writes to me all about you but I like your version
too. Love,

　　　　Penny

from the chipped chippendale desk of Penny Smith

IT'S DUTCH TREAT
ALL THE WAY AT
NEVINS MARKHAM

Store Opens Holland
Festival with 75,000
Tulips

CANYON CITY, Mar. 24 — Dressed in a special tulip print dress designed by André Laug, Mrs. Isabella Montenegro, Vice-President and Sales Promotion Director of Nevins Markham, accompanied by an old-fashioned oompah band, led 50 little Texas boys and girls dressed in Dutch costumes up the front steps of Nevins Markham to launch a tulip showing throughout the entire store. To the strains of "Tiptoe Through the Tulips," Mayor Howard Baumgarten gave the children the key to the store. Mr. Harold Nevins, President of Nevins Markham, cut the first tulips, signifying the official opening of tulip season in Holland and Canyon City.

"There are over 1,000 varieties of tulips in this exhibition, and there are 75,000 tulips in bloom here this morning," said Mr. Nevins. "They include all the most popular tulips, as well as the exotic varieties such as the Bizarres and the Van Thols. There is something in a tulip mood in every department. Tulips from Baccarat, Porthault, Fendi, Gucci, Eiseman, Delman. We have tulip lip colors and a tulip blown hair style. The store is a garden of fresh ideas and I hope everyone in Canyon City will see it."

The exhibition will continue through April 5.

For TJ Bennis

Date 3/26   **Time** 10:20

WHILE YOU WERE OUT

M Montenegro

From

Phone No.

	Area Code		Number	Extension
TELEPHONED		X	URGENT	
PLEASE CALL		X	WANTS TO SEE YOU	
WILL CALL AGAIN			CAME TO SEE YOU	
RETURNED YOUR CALL				

Message Wants you to order the tulips on hold today.

JA 3

For Mrs. Montenegro

Date 3/26   **Time** 12:45

WHILE YOU WERE OUT

M TJ Bennis

From

Phone No.

	Area Code		Number	Extension
TELEPHONED		X	URGENT	
PLEASE CALL		X	WANTS TO SEE YOU	
WILL CALL AGAIN			CAME TO SEE YOU	
RETURNED YOUR CALL				

Message Needs contact number. Rosemae has file.

I don't have it.

Rosemae

Operator

JA 3

For Sue Ellen Anderson

Date 3/26 **Time** 1 P.M.

WHILE YOU WERE OUT

M Montenegro

From

Phone No.

	Area Code		Number	Extension
TELEPHONED	**x**	URGENT		
PLEASE CALL	**x**	WANTS TO SEE YOU		
WILL CALL AGAIN		CAME TO SEE YOU		
RETURNED YOUR CALL				

Message Get contact No. on
tulip reorder to TJ
Bennis immediately.

JA 3

For Mrs. Montenegro

Date 3/26 **Time** 2 P.M.

WHILE YOU WERE OUT

M Sue Ellen Anderson

From

Phone No.

	Area Code		Number	Extension
TELEPHONED	**x**	URGENT		
PLEASE CALL		WANTS TO SEE YOU		
WILL CALL AGAIN		CAME TO SEE YOU		
RETURNED YOUR CALL				

Message All she has on tulips
is the proper crediting.

Rosemae
Operator

JA 3

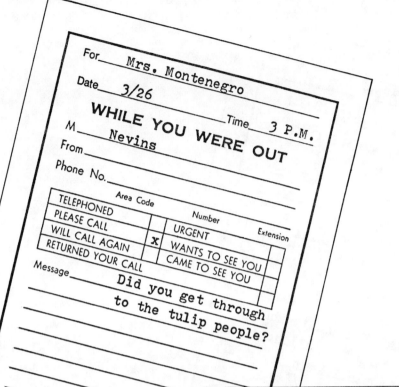

For **Mrs. Montenegro**

Date **3/26**   Time **3 P.M.**

WHILE YOU WERE OUT

M **Nevins**

From _____

Phone No. _____

	Area Code	Number	Extension
TELEPHONED			
PLEASE CALL		URGENT	
WILL CALL AGAIN	X	WANTS TO SEE YOU	
RETURNED YOUR CALL		CAME TO SEE YOU	

Message **Did you get through to the tulip people?**

JA 3   **Rosemae**
                          Operator

For **Mrs. Montenegro**

Date **3/26**   Time **4 P.M.**

WHILE YOU WERE OUT

M **Me, Rosemae**

From _____

Phone No. _____

	Area Code	Number	Extension
TELEPHONED	X	URGENT	
PLEASE CALL		WANTS TO SEE YOU	
WILL CALL AGAIN		CAME TO SEE YOU	
RETURNED YOUR CALL			

Message **No one answered at all in Haiti.**

                          Operator

JA 3

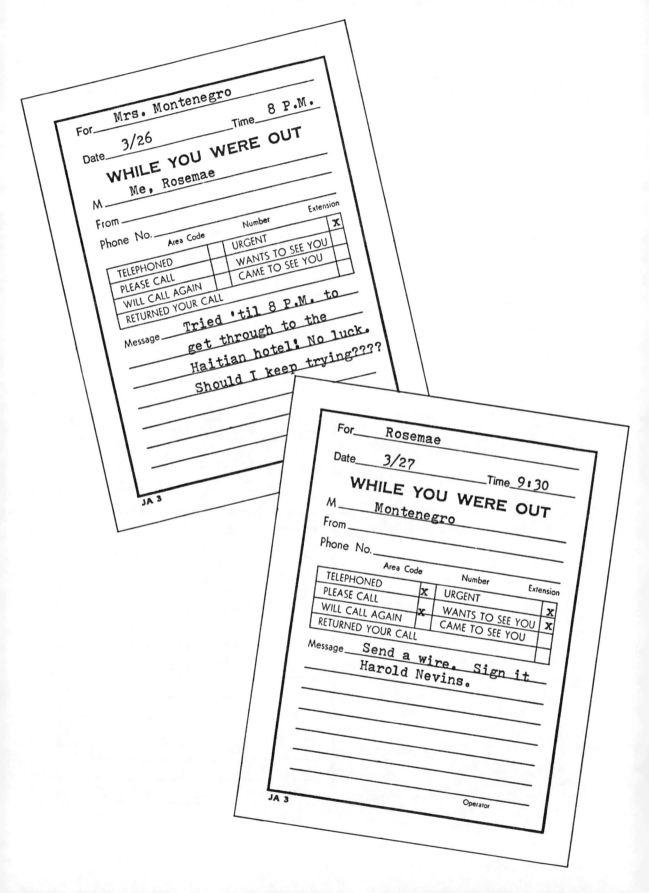

International Telegram Via

Word Count __15__ Full Rate Unless Otherwise Checked (✓)

☒ Full Rate ☐ Letter Telegram Service (LT)

Date 3/27 ☐ Other (Specify)

Sender's Name and Address

Nevins Markham
Elm & Orchard
Canyon City, Texas 78254

To

Penelope Smith
Haitian Heaven Hotel
Port-au-Prince, Haiti

 Via

ACR-ITT

insert "ITT"

If you send this blank to a Western Union
Telegraph office, insert ITT here. If you
telephone your message in, or use a desk fax
or teleprinter, insert Via ITT after the address.

Call store at once.

Harold Nevins

All messages are accepted subject to rates, rules and regulations in the
applicable tariffs on file with the Federal Communications Commission.

ITT World Communications Inc.
subsidiary of International Telephone and Telegraph Corporation

nevins markham

March 28, 1980

I fail to understand why not one person in your
entire department has either the tulip contact
name or a phone number of any kind. It was my
understanding that you yourself had made the
arrangements. The tulips are beginning to look
seedy and they will smell by Monday. I frankly think
we should salvage what remaining tulips there are,
amass them on the first floor, and quit advertising
the event immediately. I am extremely disappointed.

cc: TJ Bennis
    Sue Ellen Anderson

HN/bb

Isabella Montenegro

Vice-President/Nevins Markham
Sales Promotion

March 28, 1980

To: Harold Nevins

Indeed I did make arrangements for the
tulip promotion. Smith was to give the
tulip file to Rosemae. Rosemae has turned
the files upside down and it is simply
not there. Naturally I called my good
friend Harvey Klahorn. Unfortunately he's
in Holland for the festival. However, his
office insists that all tulips have been
shipped. I've contacted Dutch Air. They
insist they have no record. Incidentally,
Smith is not <u>in</u> Haiti. I honestly think
we should pay the piper and order
replacements which can be in the store
at 10 A.M. tomorrow. To cancel ads and
disappoint our customers is just not in
the spirit of this store.

IM/rm

Isabella Montenegro

March 28, 1980

To: TJ Bennis

I have ordered replacements of tulips
from a local wholesaler. They will be in
the store at 10 tomorrow morning. I want
everyone in Display on the job all
weekend. I want the store to look
beautiful on Monday morning.

cc: Harold Nevins

IM/rm

POST CARD

Address

N-M Advertising Dep't
Nevins Markham
Canyon City, Texas
78254

For **Mrs. Montenegro**

Date **3/31** Time **9:30**

WHILE YOU WERE OUT

M **TJ Bennis**

From

Phone No.

Area Code	Number	Extension

TELEPHONED	X	URGENT	X
PLEASE CALL	X	WANTS TO SEE YOU	
WILL CALL AGAIN		CAME TO SEE YOU	
RETURNED YOUR CALL			

Message **50,000 more tulips**
from Holland have just
arrived. Where in God's
name do I put them?

Operator

JA 3

                                                        April 1

Dearest Dar,
        I had the best time with you. It <u>was</u> Haitian heaven!
Meanwhile, back at the ranch, I got up at dawn, hit the
store, slipped back the tulip file under "Consulaat-
Generaal der Hague--tulips." I left the store. I waited 'til
8 A.M. and called the shippers to be sure they had delivered
all the tulips. Then I casually strolled into the ad
department at my usual hour. Monty was spewing flames.
        "Well," she said, "you certainly ____ed things up!"
"Me?" I said innocently. "What <u>do</u> you mean?" "I mean that
no one could lay hands on your goddamned file."
        "Oh, come on," I protested. "What's up?"
        "What's up? What's up?" she screamed. "I'll tell you
what's up. Your job! You were supposed to leave a file on
tulips. You never did. And we ran out of tulips and we
couldn't find you in Haiti, and we had to spend four grand
getting replacements, and then the damned things arrived
yesterday." She took a deep breath.
        "But Isabeyyah," I pleaded, "I <u>did</u> leave the file.
Rosemae, you remember. I gave you the Consulaat-Generaal der
Hague--tulips file."
        Rosemae burst into tears. "I don't have it!" "But it's
right here," I said incredulously as I plucked it out of the
file. "Right here under your noses. Here's everything you
needed."
        I actually felt sorry for Rosemae. She was bug-eyed. I
think Monty wanted to strangle me with her bare hands but my
ruse worked. Now everyone knows what a big phony she is and
what an idea thief she is. When I think about Rosemae, I do
feel guilty. But Monty won't fire her. She leans on her 15
hours a day. Anyway, I have tulips to take home and the store
is loaded for Mama's arrival. I cannot tell you how happy I
am. I'm mad about you. Now more than ever.
                                                Penny

from the chipped chippendale desk of Penny Smith

Isabella Montenegro

Vice-President/Nevins Markham
Sales Promotion

April 4, 1980

To: Sue Ellen Anderson
    Penelope Smith
    TJ Bennis
    Jean Derujinski

Re: Summer Sun Show

Let's put our whole tulip debacle behind
us and get on to an exciting summer. What
would all of you think about putting some
darling live animals into our show? We'll
have safari animals on blow-up slides. We
can get wonderful ones from my dear friend
Jane Chapin at Adventures Unlimited. But
for the Monkey Biz scene I see real
animals. People love animals. I know
Mr. Nevins thought the Christmas zoo was
a lot of work, but then the animals were
in the store for a month. Our event is
just a one-night stand. Smithey, why
don't you get out to the zoo and see
what's available? I want to move on this
right away, because as you all know the
show is the first week of May.

cc: Harold Nevins

IM/rm

nevins markham

elm and orchard
canyon city, texas 78254

April 7, 1980

Dr. Allan Peabody
Director
Canyon City Zoo
Canyon City, Tex.

Dear Dr. Peabody,

Nevins Markham is presenting a very special
show on May 4 on Fun and Sun clothes. We're doing
some special sections that we think the audience
will find appealing. In one segment we're doing
Summer Safaris. For this we'll do blow-up slides of
giraffes, rhinos, etc. But for one segment we wanted
to explore the possibility of getting some monkeys
for Monkey Biz. I wondered if you had any monkeys
that we could use in our show. Of course, they have
to be tame and used to people. Since yours are
certainly used to people, could you help us?

Naturally, Nevins Markham would be prepared
to make a sizable donation to the zoo for your
services.

Sincerely,

Penelope Smith
Advertising Director

PS/rm

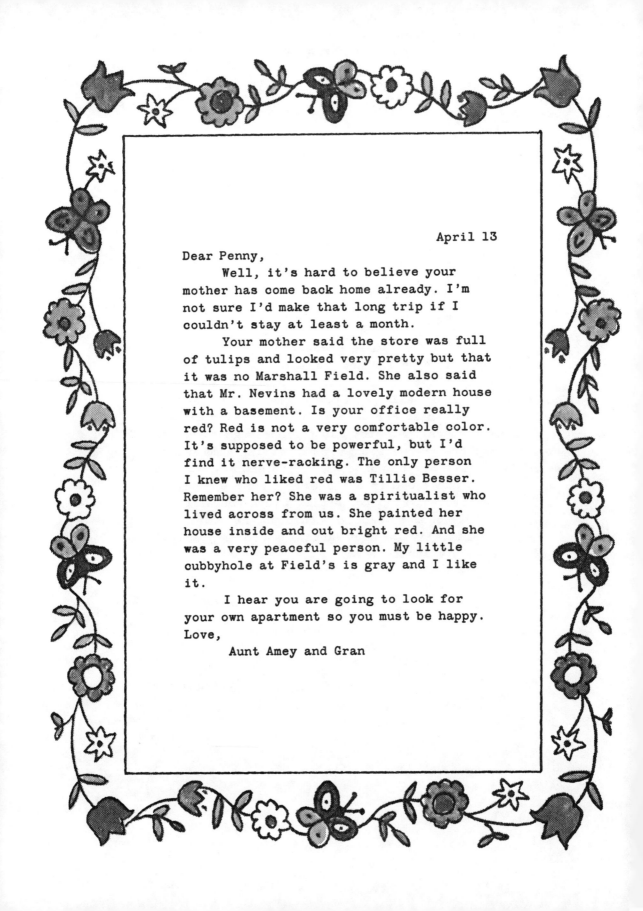

April 13

Dear Penny,

    Well, it's hard to believe your
mother has come back home already. I'm
not sure I'd make that long trip if I
couldn't stay at least a month.

    Your mother said the store was full
of tulips and looked very pretty but that
it was no Marshall Field. She also said
that Mr. Nevins had a lovely modern house
with a basement. Is your office really
red? Red is not a very comfortable color.
It's supposed to be powerful, but I'd
find it nerve-racking. The only person
I knew who liked red was Tillie Besser.
Remember her? She was a spiritualist who
lived across from us. She painted her
house inside and out bright red. And she
was a very peaceful person. My little
cubbyhole at Field's is gray and I like
it.

    I hear you are going to look for
your own apartment so you must be happy.
Love,
    Aunt Amey and Gran

Canyon City Zoo

Canyon City, Texas 78201

April 11, 1980

Ms. Penelope Smith
Advertising Director
Nevins Markham
Elm and Orchard
Canyon City, Texas 78254

Dear Ms. Smith,

   I received your letter and am delighted to help you and your store with the monkeys. We have, as a matter of fact, a very famous orangutan here in the zoo. He is tame and easy to handle and very docile. We also have five Capuchin monkeys that I think could work for you. They are very smart and do a lot of tricks on their own.

   Of course, I hate to see animals put to work for commercial ventures, but your offer of a donation to the zoo would be most welcome and I think the monkeys would have fun.

   Perhaps it might be a good idea to come out here to see for yourself what's available. If we don't have the right animals or not enough of the right animals I could put you in touch with Ed Maher of the Dallas Zoo Farm.

   The orangutan's name is Hubert. He's a remarkable beast. He's 5'5" tall and weighs about 200 pounds. He has red, shaggy hair and is quite a showman.

   Just call my office and let me know if and when you want to come for a visit. I'd be pleased to take you around.

                                  Sincerely,

                                  Allan Peabody, D.V.M.
                                  Director

AP/mm

April 14

to: Sue Ellen

How would you like to drive out to Canyon
City Zoo (not much of a change of pace
from this place)? Dr. Peabody says
he wants us to come meet Hubert the
Orangutan. He also has five Capuchins who
want to get into show biz. Maybe we could
get a snake and call the show Monty's
Python. Call me.

April 16

to: Isabella Montenegro

I checked out the zoo and I am happy to
report that you are now the proud renter
of one model-height orangutan called
Hubert and five adorable show-biz-
oriented monkeys. Dr. Peabody will come
with the animals for dress rehearsal on
May 3 at 6 P.M. Then he and his trainer
will be with the animals on May 4. I
gather Mr. Nevins will present the award
check at the end of the show. Right?
Meanwhile, I thought you'd like to mull
over these fascinating Dr. Peabodyisms:

"The orangutan is intelligent,
tractable, teachable, and swings. The
orangutan will not leap. An orangutan
walks nicely though bowlegged, and his
arms touch the floor. Hubert has 36
teeth."

nevins markham

April 18, 1980

Monkeys! That's all I need! I don't have one model
in the summer show with an IQ above 50 and you want
them to handle wild animals? None of them wants
to go along with it. I told them the animals are
harmless and friendly. Question: Do they have lice
and are lice catching?

111 NORTH STATE STREET · CHICAGO · ILLINOIS 60690 · TELEPHONE STATE 1-1000

April 20, 1980

Dear Penelope,

Aunt Amey just called to give me all the latest news. Monkeys! They're filthy beasts and quite dangerous. They bring on asthma. Aunt Amey looked up the breeds and was shocked to find out that an orangutan weighs 200 pounds. Why don't you use tropical birds?

Darwin took us all to dinner last week. It was nice of him. Why on earth don't you give up on that job and get a nice one at Field's and get married? You don't have to have children right away. I suppose you're into the women's causes. Those protesters always look so serious to me.

We went to a Chinese restaurant. It was very dark. Now I don't want you to repeat this, but Aunt Amey cut right into her steaming towel. She thought it was the first course. I would have felt foolish, but Amey passed it off like she cut into a hot towel every night.

I tried to feel Darwin out about how he'd feel about living in Canyon City but he was noncommittal.

Love,

Mother

STATE STREET · WATER TOWER PLACE · OLD ORCHARD · OAKBROOK · WOODFIELD · RIVER OAKS · HAWTHORN · FOX VALLEY
CHERRYVALE · ORLAND SQUARE · PARK FOREST · EVANSTON · OAK PARK · LAKE FOREST · MAYFAIR IN WAUWATOSA, WISCONSIN

April 23

to: Jean Derujinski

Dr. Peabody swears all his animals are
bug-free. (Yet, come to think of it,
aren't monkeys always delousing each
other?) Well, he promises to have them
all scrubbed and brushed up for the big
day. According to my mother (a monkey
gland expert), the most that can happen
to your models is that they'll have an
asthma attack. I would let Monty know,
however, that the models are unhappy. She
should get to share in all these things.

from the chipped chippendale desk of Penny Smith

nevins markham
elm and orchard
canyon city, texas 78254

May 5, 1980

Dear Mr. Nevins,

    I have had it! Despite the fact that I arranged
for the animals that we used last night in the show,
I most certainly didn't think up having Hubert and
his Capuchin orchestra. This was Mrs. Montenegro's
baby. I also told Mrs. Montenegro that I didn't
think we should dress Hubert in a Halston cape and
beret when we hadn't done so in dress rehearsal. And
that little last-minute command of hers is what
caused tame old Hubert to go bananas and leap into
the audience. I refuse to accept this buck that
Mrs. Montenegro is trying to pass. I've caught them
for a year now, and I have caught the last one. And
finally, I do not appreciate your telling me to get
Sue Ellen off the counter and out of the store.
Sue Ellen's hat dance was the only original thing
that happened last night. Sue Ellen is not my
responsibility. She's my friend. I've given this
job all I've got and I get no thanks for it. So
count me out in the future and accept this letter
as my resignation effective May 31, 1980.

        Sincerely,

        Penelope Smith

From the desk of

Sue Ellen Anderson
Public Relations/Nevins Markham

May 6, 1980

PERSONAL AND CONFIDENTIAL

To: Penny Smith

You can't quit! I think this whole thing
is out of hand. You're worse than Hubert.
I've talked to Harold and he really
does not want you to leave. Apparently
Montenegro is sorry she yelled at you in
front of all the models. You fit in here.
You do a good job. People like you.
People talk about your ads. You should at
least put in a couple more years here.
What good is one year? Have dinner with
me tonight and let's talk. Imagine what I
had to do today to keep my job. And you
are throwing yours out the window.

For Penny Smith

Date 5/7 **Time** 10:30

WHILE YOU WERE OUT

M Sue Ellen

From

Phone No.

	Area Code		Number	Extension
TELEPHONED		X	URGENT	
PLEASE CALL		X	WANTS TO SEE YOU	
WILL CALL AGAIN			CAME TO SEE YOU	
RETURNED YOUR CALL				

Message She wants to know
where you are going
and what kind of job
you'll take. She says
it's better to stay.

Rosemae
Operator

JA 3

For Sue Ellen Anderson

Date 5/7 **Time** 12:00

WHILE YOU WERE OUT

M

From Penny Smith

Phone No.

	Area Code		Number	Extension
TELEPHONED				
PLEASE CALL		X	URGENT	
WILL CALL AGAIN			WANTS TO SEE YOU	
RETURNED YOUR CALL			CAME TO SEE YOU	

Message Tell Sue Ellen I
wish I knew.

Operator

JA 3

NEVINS MARKHAM
AD DIRECTOR
RESIGNS

CANYON CITY, May 9 — Penelope Smith has resigned her post as Advertising Director of Nevins Markham, effective on May 31. She plans to make her residence in New York City. While Ad Director she was responsible for many of the advertising innovations at the store.

May 19

Dear Mama,

      Just a note to tell you your old stone is
rolling again. I resigned. I'm going to try to
get a job in an ad agency in New York. I've met
some nice people in New York and they are
helping me to relocate. I think New York is
where it's really at.

      I suppose you know Dar is furious with me.
He won't even consider changing cities. He
thinks I should grab his grandma's diamond ring
and be content. I know that you enjoy homemaking,
but I have to keep the blood in my veins rushing.
I'd go to sleep in Oak Park. I'll call and let
you know what's up. Much love,

                  The Stone

P.S. Don't say anything to Dar. I'm writing him.

from the chipped chippendale desk of Penny Smith

For **Penny Smith**

Date **5/20**   Time **10 A.M.**

WHILE YOU WERE OUT

M **Sue Ellen**

From _____

Phone No. _____

       Area Code   Number   Extension

TELEPHONED	X	URGENT	
PLEASE CALL	X	WANTS TO SEE YOU	
WILL CALL AGAIN		CAME TO SEE YOU	
RETURNED YOUR CALL			

Message **Call Sue Ellen. She has great news for you.**

_____

_____

_____

_____

_____

                     Rosemae
                       Operator

JA 3

Dar! You will never guess! Isabeyyah landed on her size 7AAA feet! She's marrying the wealthiest man in town. And the word is out that Harold is going to do everything he can now to get me to hang in. But I think I have hot things cooking in N.Y.

I really wish you'd give a lot of thought to my career. I wish I had a wife, too! Then I would have someone to live with and someone to pack my duds and meet me at the airport and have my dinner cooked for me when I get home. A wife is really a great buy.

I'll call you as soon as I hear from the ad agency in N.Y. They said they were sending me an offer. How do you feel about the Big Apple? Listen, Dar. No matter what. I do love you.

Penny

Isabella Montenegro Engaged To Lissley Jackson Cobb III

Mrs. Isabella Montenegro, the Creative Director of Nevins Markham, announced today her engagement to Lissley Jackson Cobb III, publisher of the Canyon City Clarion.

"It just happened so fast. I just up and said 'yes' to Liss's proposal. I adore Canyon City and cannot think of a place I would rather live in."

Mrs. Montenegro said that she would be leaving Nevins Markham shortly, as the pressures of being a publisher's wife would be about all she could cope with. "Being a creative director just saps your energies and I wouldn't want that to happen for either Liss or Nevins Markham."

The engaged couple plan to be married early in February, honeymoon in India, and return to the Cobb house in North Highlands, Canyon City. They will divide their time between Mr. Cobb's South American ranch and Canyon City.

from the chipped chippendale desk of Penny Smith

nevins markham

inter-office memo

to: Penelope Smith

from: Harold Nevins

May 20, 1980

Dear Penny,

Here's the <u>New York Times</u> review. The fashion editor
at the <u>Times</u> sent it on to me. I'm very pleased with
it. If you want to talk, remember my door
is <u>always</u> open.

cc: Sue Ellen Anderson

HN/bb

Delicious Reading

THE BEST OF TASTE
By Penelope Smith.
Edited by Sue Ellen Anderson.
Color illustrations. 384 pages.
New York: Harcourt Brace Jovanovich.
$18.95.

By ROGER PECCADILLO

IF you never cooked a Son of a Bitch Stew or never shouted "Hush Puppies" to the dogs of a wagon train, you simply ain't lived.

"The Best of Taste" is a compilation of recipes from Nevins Markham, supposedly the world's chicest store.

Each recipe is a regional delight with the folklore that properly accompanies it. It's well written and fun, and the author must have devoted considerable time to research. The editor is pure Texiana, and Miss Smith seems to be as much at home with Pucci's Truffles as she is with Mama's Puhcahn Pie.

The recipes were all tested by the Food and Nutrition Department of Canyon City University in Canyon City, Texas, so one feels confident that if something goes wrong it will be your fault.

If I have one criticism it's that the book's index leaves much to be desired, but the book is great fun to read and should make a nice addition to the shelf of any Texas, or for that matter American, gourmand. I can hardly wait to try the Whiskey Cake.

Mr. Peccadillo teaches third grade at Vale and is the author of "Indian Sam."

May 21,1979

To the person in
charge of the cookbook.

Nevins Markham

Elm & Orchard

Canyon City,Texas

To whom it may concern:

        I tried making your recipe for Sam

Houston's Cherry Cake, contributed by Miss

Margaret Cousins of San Antonio,Texas, on

page 364, and I want to bring to your atten-

tion that when I got all the way down to the

batter you called only for the nuts and not

for the cherries. What do I do with my

cherries? I have 2 3/4 cups of them.

        Yours very truly,

        Mrs. Hardeneda Ramsdell

Neiman-Marcus

RICHARD C. MARCUS
Chairman

May 22, 1980

Ms. Penelope Smith
687 Shinstone
Canyon City, Texas 78251

Dear Ms. Smith,

As I told you when we talked, we have been thinking
for some time now about finding a person who could
come up with special events for our suburban and
branch operations. As you know, most of the
promotional activity is pretty much in the home
store. In many instances the branches do not have
the personnel to take advantage of the excitement.
So this person must have press "savvy" as well as
promotional skills.

Over and above this, we look for originality for our
catalogues and mailings. Each year we try to top our
"his and hers gifts." Each Christmas our buyers
search for unique and exclusive items. Of course,
you'd work with our promotion team, but you would
not be involved in the day-to-day mechanics of the
job. The title we would give you could be Special
Events Director or Creative Director. We can worry
about that when you are here.

I am free next Saturday for lunch if you can
fly over. My father thought your portfolio was
excellent.

Sincerely,

Richard Marcus
Chairman

RM/dm

J. William Tooter, Inc.

477 Madison Ave.
New York, NY 10022
(212) 787-2525

May 23, 1980

Ms. Penelope Smith
687 Shinstone
Canyon City, Texas 78251

Dear Ms. Smith,

We were all very impressed with your sample
case and your qualifications. The Creative Director
has given me the "go-ahead" to make you an offer. I
know it won't seem great to you, and I know you
wanted more money, but you must take into account
that your entire background is retail-oriented and
you bring no agency expertise to the job. What
we are counting on is that you will make that
adjustment from retail thinking to agency thinking
in a year or so and that you will be able to come up
with product concepts the same way you did for store
promotions.

The best we can do would be $20,000 with a
review in six months. We would like you to work on
"Sop-ups," the new paper diaper, and "Urge," the
marvel detergent. Both of these will be going into
test markets shortly. We're putting together a
creative team on both these tests and would like to
have you aboard as soon as possible. I'd appreciate
your calling me.

I believe you will find J. William Tooter a
very happy and creative shop.

Sincerely,

Robin Belcher
Creative Services

RB/tt

                                                      May 26

Dear Mr. Nevins,

     Thank you for your very nice note. It's
flattering and most welcome. As you know, titles
mean nothing to me, but should I decide to stay I
would love to move on to Sales Promotion Director--
simply in the interest of the female image in the
advertising world.

     My dilemma is this. I've had a couple of nice
offers (N.Y. ad agency, Dallas store). The money
they offer is quite tempting. I really would like to
build a pad of my own and quit living with the night
nurse. This takes bucks. And with the cost of
living, I just have to make more money. I want you
to know that although my year here at Nevins Markham
was a tough one, it was also a fun one. I learned a
lot. I'll give your offer every consideration and
I'll let you know this week what my plans will be.
Thanks,

                         Penny

from the chipped chippendale desk of Penny Smith

A Rare Portrait of Penelope Smith at Work

Sablinka

Job Offers

OPTION CHART

Position	Salary	Advantages	Disadvantages
Sales Promo. Nevins	25 G (maybe more)	Know people Know job Know problems	None
Copywriter J. W. Tooter	20 G+	Get into agency biz. N.Y.	What happens if Sop-ups or Urge don't make it? Will I?
Creative Dir. Neiman-Marcus	25,000+	Bigger city Prestigious store	More of same in different store
Wife Darwin	0	I love him	No job Chicago
Pres. White House	200,000	Travel Power Free housing	Hate politics

from the chipped chippendale desk of **Penny Smith**

June 1

Dear Penelope,

Well, in some ways I'm sad and in some ways I'm
glad. I know you probably don't think you can handle
the job that nice lady had. But obviously they think
you can. I hope they're right. It's very hard being
demoted. Certainly that's a nice salary for someone
your age. Don't let it go to your head. Let life
be a learning experience. You've learned a lot
down there. Why, Mr. Reynoldson was amazed at your
being able to handle an orangutang. He says it takes
years of training to get an animal that size to do
anything. So we're all very proud of you.

Darwin called to say that he was flying down to
Canyon City to look over the terrain. Does that mean
he's going to buy land? If so, I hope you two will
stop living like Bohemians in Greenwich Village and
get married. I don't like the situation as it stands
at all. On the other hand, don't get your hopes up.
He may not stay.

Aunt Amey (no less) was interviewed by the
educational channel. They're doing a whole program
on Field's. Well, we all had to watch the show. All
the dishes had to be cleared off in a hurry. Amey's
part went by so fast I didn't see anything but her
ear and her hand with a slip of paper in it. But
she was thrilled to have been the first one in the
family to be on TV. You'll have to move fast to keep
apace of Aunt Amey.

Well, dear, we're all delighted you're staying
on. Of course, we would have been more delighted if
you had come home. Maybe some day Field's will offer
you the kind of job you want. Let's hope so. Well,
dear, I must close. Isn't it a shame about Charlie
Anderson living in that flat with no toilet? Love,

Mother

nevins markham

inter-office memo

to: Penny Smith, Sue Ellen Anderson

from: Hannah Nevins

June 13, 1980

Ms. Ada Pump tells me that there is a search on for
your new assistant. Might I suggest that you find
someone who can take on the top responsibility for
our Fur Storage and Remodeling Departments? This
person should have some background in the subject
and be extremely aggressive in promoting these
departments. Both Mr. Zucker and I would like to
meet with her as soon as possible.

cc: Harold Nevins

HN/ub